A STUDY OF THE TWELVE APOSTLES

12

Dr. Glenn [signature]
II Tim. 2:15

A STUDY OF THE
TWELVE APOSTLES

DR. GLENN CUMMINGS

Tate Publishing & *Enterprises*

A Study of the Twelve Apostles
Copyright © 2008 by Dr. Glenn Cummings. All rights reserved.

This title is also available as a Tate Out Loud product. Visit www.tatepublishing.com for more information.

No part of this publication may be reproduced, stored in a retrieval system or transmitted in any way by any means, electronic, mechanical, photocopy, recording or otherwise without the prior permission of the author except as provided by USA copyright law.

Scripture quotations marked "NKJV" are taken from The New King James Version / Thomas Nelson Publishers, Nashville: Thomas Nelson Publishers. Copyright © 1982. Used by permission. All rights reserved.

The opinions expressed by the author are not necessarily those of Tate Publishing, LLC.

Published by Tate Publishing & Enterprises, LLC
127 E. Trade Center Terrace | Mustang, Oklahoma 73064 USA
1.888.361.9473 | www.tatepublishing.com

Tate Publishing is committed to excellence in the publishing industry. The company reflects the philosophy established by the founders, based on Psalm 68:11,
"The Lord gave the word and great was the company of those who published it."

Book design copyright © 2008 by Tate Publishing, LLC. All rights reserved.
Cover design by Jacob Crissup
Interior design by Lynly D. Taylor

Published in the United States of America

ISBN: 978-1-60604-640-1
1. Biblical Study-Exegesis-History
2. 12 Apostles

08.10.06

ACKNOWLEDGEMENTS

This book was written to help the Christian better understand the lives of the twelve men whom Jesus called to be His Apostles. I pray it will be helpful to the individual Christian who desires to study God's Word. The format makes it easy for a discipleship class to have a 12-week study on this subject. I have included some sermons that I trust will be helpful to the pastor in preaching about these men who followed Jesus.

I dedicate this book to the following 4 preachers who have most influenced my life and ministry:

Dr. Adrian Rogers, who is now rejoicing in Heaven. What a wonderful preacher of God's Word he was!

Dr. Charles Stanley, pastor of First Baptist Church in Atlanta, GA. I began listening to you preach when I was in High School on the local TV station in Atlanta. You have now become a world-wide pastor through your "In Touch" Ministries and one of the prominent conservative leaders in our Convention. Thank you for being an example of what it means to have a pastor's heart and the courage to stand for what is right.

Dr. Jerry Vines, retired pastor of the First Baptist Church of Jacksonville, FL. I have been blessed every time I hear you preach God's Word. You are a great example of being prepared and powerfully presenting God's Word. Thank you for how you have ministered to me and thousands of pastors through the years.

Rev. Tom Suiter, IMB missionary. Bro. Tom was my pastor at Dawson Street Baptist Church in Thomasville, GA when I sensed God's call to preach. Thank you for taking the time to help me discern God's call and encouraging me to follow His will in my life.

TABLE OF CONTENTS

The Apostles of Christ | *An Overview*

9

James and John | *The Sons of Zebedee*

15

Philip | *The "Show Me" Apostle*

33

Matthew | *The Publican turned Preacher*

45

Judas Iscariot | *The Betrayer of Christ*

57

Lebbaeus Thaddaeus | *Judas, not Iscariot*

69

Simon Zelotes | *The Zealous Apostle*

81

Andrew | *The Apostle who Brought Others to Christ*

91

Peter | *The Apostolic Spokesman*

103

Thomas Didymus | *The Apostle who Had to be Sure*

117

Nathanael Bartholomew | *The Skeptical Apostle*

131

James, the Son of Alphaeus | *James the Less*

143

THE APOSTLES OF CHRIST

Introductory Study

LESSON TEXT:

Luke 6:12–16

STUDY TEXTS:

Matthew 10:2–6; Mark 3:13–19; Luke 6:12–16; Acts 1:1–4, 13–26; Acts 2:42, 43; Acts 5:12; acts 15:1–6, 22, 23; Romans 1:1–5; Romans 11:13; I Corinthians 9:1–5; I Corinthians 12:28; I Corinthians 15:5–9; II Corinthians 12:12; Galatians 2:8; Ephesians 2:20–22; Ephesians 3:3–5; Ephesians 4:11; II Peter 3:2; Jude 17; Revelation 21:14

MEMORY VERSE:

Luke 6:13–"And when it was day, he called unto him his disciples; and of them he chose twelve, whom also he named apostles;"

THE STUDY:

I. What is an Apostle?
    A. Derivation:
    The word comes from the Greek apostolos = "sent one."
    B. In This General Sense:
        1. Jesus Christ is an Apostle–Hebrews 3:1
        2. Barnabas was an apostle–Acts 14:14
        3. James, the Lord's brother (writer of the Book of James) Was an apostle–Galatians 1:19

II. The Apostolic Office:
Those who held the apostolic office were chosen from among the Disciples of Christ (Luke 6:13). There are three distinguishing "marks" of an apostle. He must have:
    A. Actually Seen Jesus Christ
        Acts 1:22; I Corinthians 15:5, 7, 8
    B. Been Personally Chosen and Audibly Called By Jesus Christ
        Matthew 10:5; Mark 3:13

  C. Been Endued With Divine Credentials (Signs)
   Mark 16:17–20; Acts 2:43, Acts 5:12;
   Hebrews 2:3, 4

The clear implication with these qualifications is that there cannot be (and are no) apostles in the 21st century (or any time since the apostolic age.) Today, there are only false apostles–II Corinthians 11:13; Revelation 2:2

III. The Apostle Paul:

It is important to note that apart from the twelve, Paul also met the above-mentioned qualifications:

  A. He Saw Christ
   I Corinthians 9:1; 15:8
  B. He Was Called
   Romans 1:1, 5; Galatians 1:1; I Timothy 2:7;
   II Timothy 1:11
  C. He Evidenced The Apostolic Signs
   II Corinthians 12:12; Acts 13:9–12; 14:8–10;
   16:16–18; 19:11,12; 28:7–9, etc.

IV. The Apostolic Office

What was the Lord's plan and purpose in calling men to be apostles?

  A. To Give Us The New Testament
   1. The Promise–John 16:13, 14
   The apostles were guided ("moved") by the
   Holy Ghost to pen the sacred text of the
   New Testament. See: II Peter 1:21
   2. The Process–Ephesians 3:1–5
   This involved the following steps:
    a. The revelation of divine Truth–verses 3, 5.
     See: Deuteronomy 29:29
    b. The recording (writing) of divine
    Truth–verse 3b–known as "inspiration."
     See: II Timothy 3:16; II Peter 1:21
    c. The retaining (preservation) of divine Truth–
    implied by the fact that God's truth was able to
    be read, verse 4 (as it still is today.)
     See: Psalm 12:6, 7; Matthew 24:35

3. The Product–II Peter 3:1, 2; Jude 17

The New Testament is the "words of the apostles and prophets!" See also: Romans 16:25, 26; II Peter 3:15, 16

B. To Establish His Churches

1. Each true New Testament Church is built upon an Apostolic Foundation–Ephesians 2:19–22 In this passage, a church is likened to a building (the temple of God.) See also: I Corinthians 12:28

2. Each true New Testament Church is built upon the Apostolic Baptism The "one baptism" (Ephesians 4:5)

a. Was instituted by Heaven through John the Baptist–John 1:6; 3:27 Matthew 21:23–27

b. Was administered by Christ through His apostles–John 3:22; 4:1, 2

c. Was authorized to the Lord's churches via the Great Commission–Matthew 28: 18, 19

Note: The church at Jerusalem required baptism as an apostolic qualification–Acts 1:22

3. Each true New Testament Church is edified by Apostolic Instruction–Ephesians 4:11–16 Ephesians 4:11–16 lists two defunct offices (apostles and prophets) that exist

Today in the New Testament scriptures and two functioning offices. Evangelists or "missionaries" and pastor-teachers) that minister today by the authority of the New Testament scriptures.

V. The Apostles of the Lamb

The twelve apostles (listed according to Matthew's arrangement) are:

1. Simon *Peter*, the son of Jona ("Barjona")

2. *Andrew* Peter, the son of Jona.

3. *James* Boanerges, the son of Zebedee– also known as James the elder

4. *John* Boanerges, the son of Zebedee

5. *Philip* (*no surname given*)

6. *Bartholomew* Nathaniel
7. *Thomas* Didymus
8. *Matthew* Levi
9. *James*, the son of Alphaeus–also known as *James the Less*
10. Lebbaeus *Thaddaeus*–also known as "*Judas, not Iscariot*"
11. *Simon*, the Canaanite–also known as "*Zelotes*"
12. *Judas Iscariot*

VI. The Life Story of the Twelve:

Note the following "stages," based on the information we know about Peter:

A. *Salvation*–circ. 25 a.d.

The apostles were all saved and baptized under the ministry of John the Baptist. This is evident from *Acts 1:22*.

In *John 1:35* and *40* we note that Andrew was a *disciple* of John the Baptist when he began to follow Jesus. Therefore he would have to be saved and baptized, since this was John's ministry.

B. *Discipleship*–circ. 26 a.d.

John 1:29–51 records a transference of the discipleship from John the Baptist to the Lord Jesus Christ. Every disciple is a believer, though (sadly) not every believer is a disciple.

C. *Call to "Full Time Service"*–circ. 27 a.d.

This occurred in *Matthew 4:18–22* and *Luke 5:27, 28*. Here the disciples actually left their profession and followed Christ all the days of their lives. Every servant of the Lord is a disciple, though not every disciple is in "full-time" service.

D. *Call to Apostleship*–circ 28 a.d.

According to *Luke 6:13*, the twelve apostles were called from within the body of full-time disciples at about the mid-point of our Lord's public ministry.

E. *Future Ministry*:

1. Peter succeeded Christ as the pastor (shepherd of the Jerusalem church–*John 21:15–17; Acts 1:15*
2. All the apostles served as pastors (bishops) in the Jerusalem church–*Acts 1:20; 4:35, 37; 6:2; Galatians 2:9*
3. Later, the apostles were distinguished from the pastors (elders) in the Jerusalem church–*Acts 15:4, 6, 22*

F. *What About Matthias and the New Jerusalem?*

1. According to *Revelation 21:14* the foundation of the New Jerusalem will be inscribed with the names of the twelve apostles of the Lamb.
  a. This would surely not include the name of Judas Iscariot
  b. Therefore, the name of Matthias will be found inscribed there–*Acts 1:25, 26*
2. There are some who hold that the church's selection of Matthias was contrary to God's will, and that the Lord's real choice as the twelfth apostle was Paul. However:
  a. The selection of Matthias met the qualifications for apostleship–*Acts 1:21, 22*
  b. The selection of Matthias was a bona fide church decision, made after prayer–*Acts 1:24, 26*
  c. The Lord has promised to ratify proper church decisions in Heaven–*Matthew 18: 17, 18*
  d. There is no repudiation of Matthias as an apostle by the Lord
  e. Paul never claimed he should have been made the twelfth apostle, and recognized the others as "apostles before me"–*I Corinthians 15:9; Galatians 1:17*

The Application:

The apostles are important to us today because of their authority. This authority is preserved in the pages of the New Testament. Matthew 28:18–20

"And Jesus came and spake unto them, saying, All power ("exousia," authority) is given unto me in heaven and in earth. Go ye therefore, and teach all nations, baptizing them in the name of the Father, and of the Son, and of the Holy Ghost: Teaching them to observe all things whatsoever I have commanded you; and, lo, I am with you always, even unto the end of the world. Amen."

The Lesson:

This is a preparatory lesson. Future lessons will examine the lives of the twelve apostles of Christ.

When teaching the material contained in this lesson, concentrate on the following points:

A. *What is an Apostle?*

Explain that these were special disciples of the Lord, chosen by Him after much prayer to do something very special. With them and through them, Jesus gave us:

    1. The New Testament
    2. The Church

B. *The Choosing Of the Twelve*

Relate the account of Jesus's choosing these special men.

C. *The Names Of the Twelve*

Challenge those you teach to memorize the names of the twelve apostles. This should be an ongoing project throughout the series.

Discussion:

The Lord Jesus Christ conducted His ministry around "concentric circles" of people–the multitudes, the disciples, the apostles, and the inner three (Peter, James and John.) What is the effectiveness of this approach in people outreach ministries? How does this principle apply to the training of upcoming leadership?

JAMES & JOHN

The Sons of Zebedee

LESSON TEXT:

Mark 10:35–45; Luke 9:46–56

STUDY TEXTS:

Matthew 4:21, 22; Matthew 10:2; Matthew 17:1; Mark 1:19, 20; Mark 3:17; Mark 9:2, 38–40; Luke 5:10, 11; Luke 9:49, 50, 54–56; John 13:23; John 21:20; Acts 12:2; I Corinthians 15:7; Galatians 2:9; Revelation 1:9, Revelation 21:2

MEMORY VERSE:

Mark 10:43–"*But so shall it not be among you: but whosoever will be great among you, shall be your minister.*"

THE STUDY:

I. The Apostles' Background:
    A. *Zebedee*
        1. Owned a family fishing business–*Matthew 4:21*
        2. Was relatively wealthy–had hired servants–*Mark 1:20*
        3. Was in partnership with Peter and Andrew–*Luke 5:10*
    B. *James*
        1. James is the English form of Jacob = "*supplanter.*"
        2. There are *three* different James in the New Testament:
            a. James, the son of Zebedee. By comparing *Matthew 27:56* with *Mark 15:40; 16:1* we can determine that his mother's name was Salome.
            b. James, the son of Alphaeus–another apostle also known as "James, the Less" (*Matthew 10:3*). His mother's name was Mary, *Mark 15:40*.
            c. James, the step-brother of the Lord–*Matthew 13:55*. His mother's name was obviously Mary. After the death of the Apostle James, this James

became the presiding elder (pastor) of the Church at Jerusalem. *Acts 12:17; 15:13; 21:18; Galatians 1:19*.

He also was the human writer of the Book of James.

3. There is no recorded statement (quote) by James in the Bible. He has been called the 'Quiet Apostle."

4. James was the third martyr–*Acts 12:2*. John the Baptist was the first Christian martyr, Stephen was the second.

C. *John*

1. Probably the youngest of the apostles.

2. John was the last apostle to die (c. 96 a.d.) possibly the only one to die of natural causes–albeit in exile (*Revelation 1:9*)

3. There are three other Johns mentioned in the New Testament:

    a. John the Baptist–*Matthew 3:1*

    b. John Mark–*Acts 12:12, 25; 13:5, 13; 15:37*

    c. A Jewish Leader–*Acts 4:6*

4. John evidently had a very close relationship with His Lord–*John 13:23; 21:20*

5. John was entrusted with the care of Mary, the mother of Jesus–*John 19:25-27*

6. John later associated with the churches in Asia Minor–*Revelation 1:11*

7. John was the human writer of five New Testament books:

    - The Gospel of John

    - The three Epistles of John (I, II, & III John)

    - The Book of Revelation

D. *The Two Brothers*:

1. James was undoubtedly the eldest because he is always mentioned first.

2. Jesus nicknamed them the "sons of thunder"–*Mark 3:17*. This was because of their disposition.

3. Both were members of the "inner circle"–*Matthew 17:1; Mark 5:37; Mark 13:3; Mark 14:33*.

II. The Apostles' Disposition:

James and John were not called "the sons of thunder" without good reason. They no doubt possessed quite an explosive *temper*. This is exhibited by the following negative character traits:

- A. *Jealousy*

    Read: *Mark 9:38–41; Luke 9:49.50*

    1. Not everyone will serve the Lord where and how you might think they ought. Consider: *Matthew 20:1–16; Philippians 1:15–18; and the case of Apollos in Acts 18:24–26.*
    2. A party spirit in a church is divisive.
    See: *I Corinthians 1:11–13, 3:3–7*

    Note: This does not mean that we cannot or should not speak out against unscriptural men and methods, or those who would pervert the truth of the Word of God (*Romans 16:17; Jude 3, 4.*) In His rebuke to James and John, the Lord Jesus Christ indicates that the one they were trying to stop was also serving Him faithfully–just not in the way they thought he should.

- B. *Intolerance*

    Read Luke 9:51–56

    1. Our task is to faithfully preach the Gospel to every creature–*Acts 13:46*.
    2. God is the One Who will "settle the score"–*Romans 12:18–21; II Thessalonians 1:4–10.*

- C. *Ambition*

    Read: *Mark 10:35–45; Matthew 20:20–28*

In this passage, the Lord gives a lesson on what *ministry* is all about.

   1. *The Ministry according to Mother–Matthew 20:20, 21*
       a. What Mother doesn't want the best for her children? Yet how often do worldly ambitions on the part of parents keep their children from serving God?!
       b. James and John were in on this request–*Mark 10:35*. To them, the ministry had to do with *position*.
       c. Jesus responded by speaking about the "baptism" of suffering (being overwhelmed, immersed in death.)
   2. *The Ministry according to Man–Matthew 20:25*

> a. This view of the ministry sees it as one of power.
> b. Pastors have power authority, but it is a delegated authority and must be used as such–I Peter 5:2–5. cf. II John 9, 10.
>
> 3. *The Ministry according to the Master–Matthew 20:26–28*
>   a. True ministry is one of *privilege* to serve others–*Matthew 23:10–12*
>   b. It is what the Lord became *for* us–*Philippians 2:5–8*
>   c. It is what the Lord is looking for *in* us–*Matthew 25:21, 23*
>   d. It is what we are usually least best at–*Luke 17:10*
>   e. Paul called himself a "servant" *['doulos'–bond-slave]* of Jesus Christ"–*Romans 1:1;* etc.

III. The Apostles' Transformation:

What was it that changed these brawny fishermen from hot-tempered, opinionated, bigoted, ambitious men into two of the greatest apostles of the Lamb?

> A. *They Were Changed*!
>
> > 1. *James* was the first of the twelve to "drink the cup" of death–*Acts 12:2*. Gone was any ambition for lofty position.
> > 2. *John* became the apostle of love. The word "love" is found over 60 times in John's writings. Gone was any quick-tempered reaction toward others who didn't conform to his ways. In his Gospel, the name John is not found. Instead, John identifies himself as the one *"whom Jesus loved."*
> > 3. *Both* men (serving as apostles and pastors of the church at Jerusalem) were identified by the newly converted Saul of Tarsus as men who *"seemed to be pillars"–Galatians 2:9*. There was no pretentious display of their position or authority.
>
> B. *How Were They Changed?*

It was a matter of "caught rather than taught." Time spent with Christ always changes one's life!

The Master was their example of:

> > 1. *Love–John 15:13; I John 3:16; 4:10* John learned love by being loved.

2. Humility–Matthew 20:28

THE APPLICATION:

The path to greatness in the eyes of the Lord is via the "servant's entrance." The Lord takes special note of what we do (*Romans 16:4a*) and what we don't do (*Nehemiah 3:5b.*). The Lord takes us as unprofitable servants and seeks to change us into profitable ones (*II Timothy 4:11*).

THE LESSON:

A. *Relate The Story of James & John*
   1. Their life as fishermen on the Sea of Galilee.
   2. How Jesus called them to be "fishers of men"–*Matthew 4:19*
   3. How Jesus made them into fishers (instead of "nukers") of men–*Matthew 4:19*
   4. How they went on to serve their Lord with their lives.

B. *Teach About the Problems James and John Had in Their Lives*
   1. Show how these things are a detriment to service
   2. Explain how Jesus changed these two men
   3. Highlight how Jesus can and wants to transform us.

C. *Conclude With The Lord's Lesson on Humility*
   1. Teach and explain the memory verse
   2. Review the names of the twelve apostles

DISCUSSION:

- What are some practical ways we can serve the Lord (and others) in our Church?
- Jesus Christ is the greatest example of servanthood there is.
- How does the average church member measure up to His example (How do I measure up?)
- John was the youngest of the apostles, possibly an older teen when he first began following Christ.
- What are the characteristics of youthful exuberance (in relationship to the Christian life?)
- What is the danger with emotionally driven responses to situations in life?

- In what way are impulsiveness and overly cautious inaction dangerous extremes?
- Distinguish "reacting" versus "responding."
- How does the lesson illustrate the following?
- "God 'believes in you,' and accepts you as a person of worth and value!"
- Love is the strongest force for change.

John

Sermon Title: The Disciple of Love

John 13:23

In this message we are considering the disciple who is perhaps the best known and the best loved of all the disciples. He was a man of outstanding character. He was a man who enjoyed an intimate relationship with Jesus. He was a man who was a part of Jesus's inner-most circle with Peter and who was a part of Jesus's inner-most circle with Peter and James. He was a man who served his Lord longer than any of the other 12. He was a man who wrote more of the New Testament than any other person with the exception of the Apostle Paul and maybe Luke. John wrote a gospel, three epistles and the Apocalypse or the Revelation of Jesus Christ. His name was John and he was the brother of the other disciple we have studied in this chapter named James, the Son of Zebedee.

John was as rough and rugged, hard-headed and hard-edged as any of the other fisherman disciples. He could be as ambitious and intolerant as James. He could be as explosive as Peter. As a matter of fact, the only time that Matthew, Mark, or Luke record John speaking for himself, He's telling Jesus how he just ripped into a person who wasn't a follower of Jesus for casting out demons in Jesus's name–and half-way bragging to Jesus about it. Another time, he's right in there with his brother James asking Jesus to let them call fire down out of heaven to destroy some Samaritans who'd just rejected Jesus. He was right there when his mother was asking Jesus to let her boys sit on His right hand and on his left when He came into His kingdom. He even said that he was able to drink of the cup that Jesus was about to drink–speaking of His death.

So, as you read the Bible, it's clear that John could be just as narrow-minded and hard-headed, just as egotistical and explosive, just as aggressive and ambitious as his older brother James was.

But here's the thing–John aged well. He matured. As he grew older he didn't become bitter, he became better. The Holy Spirit molded him and made him into the man that the Lord desired that he should be.

As a matter of fact, if you compare the young man that is presented in his gospel with the old man that's found in the Revelation, you'll see that he had matured personally, as well as spiritually. You'll find that all of his liabilities were traded for assets, and that his glaring weaknesses had been turned into his greatest strengths. Just like the Bible says in 2nd Corinthians 12:9, *the Lord's strength had truly been made perfect in his weakness.*

Now, don't misunderstand, John was still John, he still had the same personality and the same gifts and the same abilities, but he had been transformed into the John that Jesus desired him to be. Like that great English Philosopher John Locke said, "When God makes a prophet, He doesn't unmake the man."

Now, whenever anybody thinks about John, they normally and naturally associate him with the word Love. As a matter of fact, he's known universally as "the apostle of love," and there are several reasons for that. First of all, his name means "whom Jehovah loves." Secondly, he's referred to in our text for this message as *"the disciple whom Jesus loved."* It says in *John 13:23*, "Now there was leaning on Jesus's bosom one of His disciples, *whom Jesus loved."* And theologians and Bible scholars have overwhelmingly and traditionally said that this was none other than the disciple of John. Now, Jesus loved all of those He had chosen, but somehow Jesus loved John as He loved His own soul. Again, you might say that John became a man after Jesus's own heart.

One of the major themes of his writings is love. More than 80 times in his gospel, epistles and the Revelation, John uses the word "love." But here's what I want you to understand–when John uses the word "love" it is not just an emotion, it is a principle, it's a power, it's a life-changing, person-transforming virtue that comes from God Himself. John even wrote in his first letter, *"He who does not love does not know God, for God is love."* And it was that divine principle and that heavenly power that transformed him from "the son of thunder" to "the disciple of love."

As one commentator put it, "The whole teaching of John on love is vibrant with the deep heart-knowledge and experience of one who had sounded its depths."

In His Gospel, John Experienced a Sentimental Love

You can sense it in his writing; you can see it as he lay his head on the chest of Jesus. John had a sentimental, emotional love for Jesus. Now, I want to say this—there's nothing wrong with an emotional, sentimental *love. All* love has to start somewhere, but an emotional love is an immature love. It has power, but no boundaries. It has strength, but no control. And you sense this in John in his gospel. He's a hot-head with a hot-heart.

Ephesians says that as Christians we are not just to speak the truth, but we are to speak the truth in love.

Listen, truth without love has no decency; it's just brutality. But on the other hand, love without truth has no character; it's just hypocrisy. That's what I learn from reading about John's love for Jesus in his gospel. He wanted to be near Jesus. He wanted to hear Jesus's heart. He wanted to have that equal, but special, relationship with Jesus. Can you imagine what it must have been like to lay your head on the chest of the One who created this world and came to die for this world? Can you imagine what it must have been like for this young disciple, probably the youngest of the twelve, to be called *"the disciple who Jesus loved?"* It must have stirred his heart. It must have put him on cloud nine. It must have kept him up at night, this tremendous emotional, sentimental love that he had for his Lord.

As a matter of fact, the word that is used three times in John's gospel, when he refers to himself as the disciple whom Jesus loved is the word, *phileo*. It's the word that speaks of a brotherly love. In a lot of ways, it is an immature love. I say that because when Jesus asked Peter, *"Do you love me?"* in *John 21* He used the word "agape" which means "unconditional, Christ-like love." But the first two times that Peter answers that question he uses the word *phileo* which again means "brotherly love." And so, on the third time, Jesus changes from agape—unconditional love to *phileo*—brotherly love, and when he does that Peter says, "Yes, I love you with a brotherly love." You see, Peter had blown it. He had messed up and he knew that his love wasn't where it was supposed to be. It wasn't mature, it wasn't agape, but when Jesus brought the concept down to brotherly love, Peter jumped all over it and said, "Yes, I love you like a brother." It's an emotional, sentimental love.

Think about this. What would our churches, families, and believers be like if we loved Jesus the way that John did? What would our churches, families, and believers act like if they love Jesus the way that John did? Do you think we'd have to twist their arms or promise them this gift or that gadget in order to get them to read their Bible or spend time alone with Jesus in prayer? Do you think that we'd have to stay on them week after week, encouraging and exhorting them to come to church and worship Him? Listen, there's a reason why John is known as the "apostle of Love" and that is because he loved. He loved Jesus. He loved His church and he loved everybody else who loved Him as well.

In His Epistles, John Expresses a Surrendered Love

Just look at what John said about love in his letters:

1st John 2:5, *"But whoever keeps His word, truly the love of God is perfected in him. But this we know that we are in Him."*

1st John 2:15, *"Do not love the world or the things in the world. If anyone loves the world, the love of the Father is not in him."*

1st John 3:18, *"My little children, let us not love in word or in tongue, but in deed and in truth."*

1st John 4:17, *"Love has been perfected among us in this: that we may have boldness in the day of judgment; because as He is, so are we in this world."*

1st John 5:3, *"For this is the love of God, that we keep His commandments. And His commandments are not burdensome."*

You see, when John wrote his gospel, he was a young man, but as he picks up his pen to write his pastoral letters, He's got the experience of age, he's matured and developed, and grown in his understanding of what love is. It's no longer just a sentiment, its surrender. All throughout these three little letters, he keeps reminding his "little children" of the importance and the impact and the imperative of surrendered love.

Now, why do I call this a surrendered love? Well, because he begins by saying that if you don't keep Christ's commandments, you can't say that you love Him. And then he even says that those people who keep His Word have the love of God perfected or matured in them. That's quite a change from the writings of the young man in his gospel. It's moved from the emotional to the volitional, from the feelings to the will.

An immature love lives for self, what self can get, but a surrendered love lives for the Savior, what the self can give. That's why I believe that so many people in our churches are still living and operating on the basis of a sentimental, and a somewhat selfish love. They want to be near Jesus, they just don't want to have to obey Jesus. They want all of the benefits without having any of the burdens, and yet John had come to the point and place in his life where he could write, *"His commandments are not burdensome."*

In The Revelation, John Exhibits A Sacrificial Love

Listen to what the elder statesman of the church writes as he begins one of the greatest books in the entire Bible. Revelation 1:9, *"I, John, both your brother and companion in the tribulation and kingdom and patience of Jesus Christ, was on the island that is called Patmos for the word of God and for the testimony of Jesus Christ."*

When Tony Dungy was coaching the Tampa Bay Buccaneers, he had a defensive end named Warren Sapp who played for him. Warren Sapp is an immense man who loves Tony Dungy, and one time while he was trying to express his feeling for Dungy he said, "I'd take a bullet for him... if it wouldn't kill me."

When Pearl Harbor was bombed, one of the Americans who volunteered to serve his country was Bob Feller. Bob was a 23-year old pitcher for the Cleveland Indians, a phenomenon who had already pitched a no-hitter and won 107 games in the major leagues. Bob was reaching his peak years as an athlete, but he gave up those years to shoot down planes in the Pacific. When he returned to baseball, after serving his country, Bob went on to throw three no-hitters, 12 one-hitters, and win 26 games.

But his years of military service–during which he could have won another 80–100 games–cost Bob much of the fame that he deserved. When baseball fans elected the All-Century team in 1999, Bob and his 266 victories were ignored in favor of two other pitchers, Christy Mathewson and Lefty Grove. Some suggest Feller may be the most underrated baseball player of all time.

Feller was once asked if he regretted his wartime service. "No." he said. "I've made many mistakes in my life. That wasn't one of them."

It is never a mistake when you give up some worldly possessions and pleasures to serve the Lord. The more we love Him, the less we will have an attachment to this world.

James

Sermon Title: The Son of Zebedee

Mark 3:13–17

In this message, we are going to be looking at and learning about the person and the passion of a man by the name of "James, the son of Zebedee." I probably need to stop here for a moment and make a clarification. You see, there are three main characters in the New Testament who were named James. So, this wasn't the James who was the half-brother of Jesus, the James who wrote the letter that we now call the book of James, and who served as the pastor of the church in Jerusalem. Neither was he the other "James, the son of Alphaeus" who was also an apostle and most likely Matthew's brother. This was "James, the son of Zebedee."

Of the three men who were in Jesus's inner-circle, we probably know less about this man by the name of James than any of the others. Because as you study the Bible there are basically no explicit details of his life and personality; whenever he is mentioned in the gospels he's always tied together to his younger and better-known brother, John, and just to be honest, the only time that James is mentioned in the Bible by himself is when we are told that he was beheaded at the command of Herod Agrippa. And even then he's referred to as John's brother.

And yet, the times that we see James in the pages of scripture, there is one thing that you can't get away from, and that is the fact that there was a confidence and a passion and a zeal to his personality that is very compelling and convicting to read about even today. As a matter of fact, it was this part of his person that probably caused Jesus to name him and John "the sons of thunder."

Look in Mark chapter 3, beginning in verse 13. This is one of the 3 main lists that detail for us the names of the twelve men that Jesus chose to follow Him and fulfill his mission and ministry upon this earth, and the Bible tells us...

"And he goeth up into a mountain, and calleth unto him whom he would:

and they came unto him. ¹⁴And he ordained twelve, that they should be with him, and that he might send them forth to preach, ¹⁵And to have power to heal sicknesses, and to cast out devils: ¹⁶And Simon he surnamed Peter; ¹⁷And James the son of Zebedee, and John the brother of James; and he surnamed them Boanerges, which is, The sons of thunder:"

In these verses, we see where these men went from being disciples, those who followed Jesus, to apostles, those sent out from Jesus.

These two brothers were the "disciples of thunder–the sons of thunder." Now what does that mean? What did Jesus mean when He gave this nickname to the two sons of a fisherman by the name of Zebedee? Was it a compliment? Probably not. Was it a reminder or a reprimand like nicknaming Simon "Peter?" Probably. Did it say something abut their actions, their attitudes, their affections, or their ambitions? Absolutely. But, even if that was the case, the question still remains, "What did Jesus mean when He called him and his brother, "Sons of thunder?"

I believe it was because he shook the world with his forceful faith in Jesus. He personified Hebrews 12:26 where it talks about a voice shaking the heavens and the earth.

I love the powerful, rhetorical question that Herbert Lockyer asked about him and his nickname, "Did such a new name or nickname reveal that they had been men of a fiery, impetuous disposition? Well, because Jesus knew what was in man, He knew all about the natural disposition of James, and set abut not its eradication but it sanctification. He harnessed the Niagara Falls in James to make him a driving force in His Kingdom."

And so, as we look at James, we gather that he had an all-consuming zeal and a passion for Jesus that must have vibrated in his voice and shown on his face. He couldn't do anything half-way, or shoddy for his Savior, and in that he was only rivaled by one other disciple, Simon Peter. This probably explains why they were always mentioned first. Everything that he was and everything that he had, his body and his soul and his spirit, was laid out as an offering for his Lord both in his life and in his death. And so, there are so many positive things that we can see in and say about James, but the main thing that I want you to catch in this message is that if a fisherman from Galilee can shake the world by his faith in Jesus, so can you and I.

Here's the first thing that I want you to see about James, the son of Zebedee, and his faith that shook the world.

His Early Life

Now James had an early, earthly life before he ever met Jesus and was called to follow Him. I get the feeling that a lot of times we tend to view these men in a vacuum. A lot of times, I think that people get the idea that these men just kind of showed up on the scene out of nowhere. Jesus picked real, ordinary, everyday run of the mill men to follow Him and to become His disciples. He knew their faults and their failures. He knew their strengths and their shortcomings. He knew their personalities and their potential. Jesus knew everything about them, and in spite of that, or maybe even because of those very things, He called them to follow Him. And one of those whom He called to follow Him was an ordinary man by the name of James.

Now, who and what was James, the son of Zebedee, when Jesus called him? What does the Bible tell us about him? He was a fisherman. He was called on the same day and really at the same place that Peter and Andrew and his brother John were called. They kind of had a fishing partnership together (*Matthew 4:18–10*).

His father's name was Zebedee, a prosperous fisherman and an influential religious and political leader from Galilee. Zebedee was known as a friend of the High Priest, Caiaphas, and his family. The Bible tells us that Zebedee had servants that helped him in the management and the operation of his fishing boats.

His mother's name was Salome. There are some who believe that she was a sister of Jesus's mother, Mary, which would help us in understanding why she did some of the things that she did and said some of the things that she said. This would also make James a physical cousin of Jesus.

His name means "supplanter" which means "one who grabs at the sole or the foot of another." It's the idea of somebody who's trying to trip up the person in front of them in order to get ahead of them. This might explain why his mother asked Jesus to let her two boys sit on his right and left hands when he came into His Kingdom. He was being pushed to be preeminent.

Evidently, he was like dynamite. He had a short fuse and when he exploded the effects were devastating. Have you ever noticed how God has a way of taming a terrible temper? That's just one of the personal problems that James had to deal with, and ultimately overcome through the Spirit's power, in order for Jesus to use him the way He wanted to.

So, the thing that I want you to understand as we look at his early life is that here was an ordinary man, with everyday issues (one of which was a terrible temper), who was transformed into a dedicated disciple of the Lord Jesus.

His Explosive Love

Have you ever heard somebody make the statement, "Well, I'm a lover, not a fighter?" Hey, when it came to James, he was both. You see, the thing that made him go to such extremes at times was the fact that he loved with such a red, hot, passionate love.

Like one philosopher put it, "Passion is the wind that fills the sails of the vessel; they sink it at times, but without them it would be impossible to make way."

That's the way James was. He was either for something 100% or he was against something 100%. He didn't do anything half-way. Can't you imagine what it must have been like for Salome, the mother of James and John, when they were growing up? I can just hear her now, "James and John, you stop fighting right this instant! I'll tell you what, I just can't take you two boys anywhere." And the next minute they'd be playing together like best friends, which evidently they were, because whenever you see them on the pages of Scripture, they're always together. As a matter of fact, most Bible scholars believe that when Jesus sent them out two-by-two that James and John probably went out together.

Now, we've seen what he was and where he was before he followed Jesus, but what about after he made that decision to drop his nets and commit his life to Christ? What does the Bible tell us about him at this point in his life?

Well, again, for one thing, in the gospels he's never alone. He's always listed with his brother John in the three main lists of disciples that we've mentioned.

He was in Jesus's inner-circle, along with Peter and John, and was allowed to see and be a part of things that nobody else ever did. He was there when Jesus raised Jairus's daughter from the dead. He was there to witness Jesus's glory on the Mount of Transfiguration. He was among four disciples to question Jesus in private on the Mount of Olives. And he was included again with John and Peter when the Lord asked them to personally pray for Him in the Garden of Gethsemane.

As a member of the small inner circle, he was privileged to witness Jesus's power in the raising of the dead, he saw His glory when Jesus was transfigured, he saw Christ's sovereignty in the way the Lord unfolded the future for them on the Mount of Olives, and he saw the Savior's agony in the garden.

He was definitely a man of action, not a man of words, because as far as we know Scripture doesn't give us any words that he spoke or wrote, unless Acts 4:24–30 be the exception.

Like Peter, he was often opening up his mouth and sticking his foot in it. I guess other than having the Savior nickname you a son of thunder, the best example of this is found in Luke chapter 9. Jesus was going to go to Jerusalem for the Passover and he decided to pass through Samaria. The shortest route from Galilee to Jerusalem went right through Samaria, but most Jews went through the barren desert of Perea, which meant that they had to go many, many miles out of the way, cross the Jordan River twice, just to keep from going to go through Samaria. So, needless to say, this was a big deal that Jesus, a Jew was going to go through Samaria. But listen to what *Luke 9,* verses *51–53* says, *"Now it came to pass, when the time had come for Him to be received up, that He steadfastly set His face to go to Jerusalem, and sent messengers before His face. And as they went, they entered a village of the Samaritans, to prepare for Him. But they did not receive Him, because His face was set for the journey to Jerusalem."*

This wasn't the first time that Jesus had gone through Samaria. He had always treated them kindly and with respect, which was more than you could say about other Jews who referred to them as "dogs." But, in spite of that, they wouldn't receive Him, they rejected Him.

So, look at what James and John decide would be the best course of action for Jesus. Verse 54, *"And when His disciples James and John saw this, they said, Lord do You want us to command fire to come down from heaven and consume them, just as Elijah did?"* There's Christian love for you.

Now, theologically and historically, there are all kinds of significance in that statement. Again, the Jews couldn't stand the Samaritans, so there was more than a little bit of prejudice here. Samaria was associated with pagan worship, so the idea of calling down fire like Elijah did on the prophets of Baal was a pretty good analogy. But there is a personal significance in that statement as well. James loved Jesus, and the idea of somebody mistreating Jesus or rejecting Jesus was unacceptable. Again, if James was for you, he was for you, but if he was against you, he was against you.

Do you remember when Jesus made this statement? *"If anyone comes to Me and does not hate his father and mother, wife and children, brothers and sisters, yes, and his own life also, he cannot be My disciple."* Do you remember that statement? Of course, what Jesus meant there was that your love for Him has to be so great that it makes your love for everybody else in comparison look like hate. Well, James must have taken that to heart, because he loved Jesus.

Do you love Jesus like James? Do you love Him more than your family? Do you love Him more than your friends? Do you love Him more than your finances or even your future? James did. He loved Him with a red, hot, passionate, all-consuming love. He even loved Him enough to go the ultimate distance and love Jesus more than his own life.

Turn to Act 12, and let me show you the last thing that I want you to see about this son of thunder.

His Enduring Legacy

Look at Acts 12, verse 1. *"Now about that time Herod the king stretched out his hand to harass some from the church. The he killed James the brother of John with the sword."* His mother had asked Jesus to give her boys a special place in His kingdom, and Jesus responded by saying to them, *"You do not know what you ask. Are you able to drink the cup that I am about to drink, and be baptized with the baptism that I am baptized with?"* They said to Him, *"We are able."* So He said to them in verse 23, *"You will indeed drink My cup, and be baptized with the baptism that I am baptized with; but to sit on My right hand and on My left is not Mine to give, but it is for those for whom it is prepared by My Father."*

The cup and the baptism of pain and death were his. Seventeen years after he accepted the call to follow Jesus, James was beheaded by Herod Agrippa. He was the second of the martyrs and the first of the apostles to give his life for Christ.

But like Jim Elliot, the missionary who was martyred by South American Indians in the 1950s said, "He is no fool who gives what he cannot keep to gain what he cannot lose."

What a great example James gave us in a passion to love and serve God in our day.

PHILIP

The "Show Me" Apostle

LESSON TEXT:

John 6:3–13

STUDY TEXTS:

Matthew 10:3; Mark 3:18; Luke 6:14; John 1:43–46; John 6:3–7; John 12:20–24; John14: 6–10; Acts 1:14

MEMORY VERSE:

John 14:8–*"Philip saith unto Him, Lord, show us the Father, and it sufficeth us."*

THE STUDY:

I. Philip's Background:
    A. *His Name*: Philip (Greek: *philippos*) = "lover of horses."
    B. *His Distinction*: The apostle is one of *three* Philips mentioned in the New Testament. The other two are:
        1. *Philip the tetrarch* of Ituraea and Trachonitis–*Luke 3:1*
        2. *Philip the deacon* (*Acts 6:5*) who became Philip the Evangelist (*Acts 21:8*)
        Notice he is distinguished from "the twelve" (*Acts 6:2*)
        The exploits of this Philip are recorded in *Acts 8*
    C. *His Birthplace*: Philip came from Bethsaida, a fishing village at the top of the Sea of Galilee– *John 1:44*
        Philip was no doubt well acquainted with Peter and Andrew.
    D. *Notes Of Interest Concerning The Apostle Philip*:
        1. Apart from his inclusion in the listings of the twelve apostles (*Matthew 10:3; Mark 3:18; Luke 6:14* and *Acts 1:14*) all that we know about Philip is recorded in the Gospel of John
        2. Nothing is said about the apostle Philip after *Acts 1:14*

3. Legendary accounts have Philip preaching in Asia Minor where he was later martyred.

  4. Philip is noted for his *analytical* (the "why") and *practical* (the "how") approach to the things of God

II. Philip Becomes A Disciple Of Christ:

Read: *John 1:43–46*

Some Galilean disciples of John the Baptist were with him in Bethabara (near the north end of the Dead Sea) when he introduced them to Christ. *John 1:35–51* relates how they left off following John and became disciples of Jesus. The first two men to do so were Andrew and an unnamed disciple (probably John). Andrew found Peter his brother and introduced him to the Saviour. The day following, as Jesus was preparing to travel to Galilee, He called Philip to follow Him. Here we note the two-fold basis of Philip's discipleship:

A. *The Word of God*

See: *verse 45*

Philip was not one to follow blindly. He wanted to see it in the Scriptures before he would believe. This is a noble attribute, worthy of all true disciples– *Acts 17:11; John 5:39*

Faith is not a leap in the dark–it's a leap in the Book!

Note the order in *Hebrews 1:13*:

1. Received the promises
2. Persuaded of them
3. Embraced them
4. Confessed

See also: *II Timothy 1:12b*

("know"–"believed"–"persuaded"–committed")

Pastors are to be followed, but not blindly! *"Whose FAITH follow"– Hebrews 13:7.* We only follow the man as he preaches the Word.

B. *Personal Experience*

See: *verse 46d–"come and see."*

Salvation by faith produces a personal experience–*Psalm 34:8*. A new life *(John 16:24,)* spiritual blessings of all kinds *(Ephesians 1:3,)* etc., are all part of the Christian experience. They are evidence of God's work of grace–*John 9:25*

Note: Experience must *always* remain

secondary to the Word of God. God's order is: *fact (Acts 8:32)–faith (Acts 8:39d)*

III. Philip Discovers The Power Of Christ:

Read: John 6:3–13

In this passage, the Lord Jesus deals with Philip's practical approach:

A. *The Lord's Question*

Notice that Jesus specifically asked Philip this question, *"Whence shall we buy bread, that these may eat?"–verse 5*

B. *The Lord's Purpose*

This was to "prove" (test) Philip–*verse 6*. He knew Philip was practical minded and would want to 'figure it out" first. If a bread roll cost 20 cents, it would cost at least $1,000 to feed 5,000 men, not to mention any women and children!–*verse 10*. Philip had it all figured out–it couldn't be done! Evidently the disciples could come up with 200 pennies between them (*verse 7)* but that would only be enough to take care of them!

C. *The Lord's Lesson*

It is good to be practical (*Luke 14:31)* so long as that practicality takes into account God's Word. *Faith* (i.e., acting on the Word of God) always supersedes practical reasoning. On this occasion, it was the Lord's will to feed the multitude. Therefore, reason became meaningless. There is an important balance to be learned here.

Example: The Bible commands our Church to "go into *all* the world and preach the Gospel to *every* creature" (*Mark 16:15)*. Reason would say, "That's impractical. It's impossible! It can't be done!" Faith would say, *"With God, all things are possible." (Mark 10:27.)* The key to this matter is always the Word of God. If God has clearly spoken, reason won't always work, but faith will. Philip surely learned that day that his practical approach had to include God. The miracle of the feeding of the 5,000 men is the only miracle of Christ to be recorded in each of the four Gospels–*Matthew 14:13–21; Mark 6:33–44; Luke 9: 1–17* and *John 6:2–13*. It is interesting to note some different approaches we might adopt when confronted with a great obstacle. Christ wanted to minister to the multitude–just as he wants us to reach the world with the Gospel.

We could:
- Send the multitude away *(Matthew 14:15)*. But how shall they hear without a preacher *(Romans 10:15)*?
- Blame the multitude for not bringing their own food. But if they believe not, they shall die in their sins *(John 8:24)*.
- Ignore the multitude and hope they will go away. But if we fail to warn them, their blood will be required at our hand *(Ezekiel 33:8)*.
- Run from the multitude. But there will be another 4,000 + to face later *(Matthew 15:32–39)*.
- Deal with the multitude by faith. Our task is to preach Christ. God's task is to save, regenerate, and perform the miracle.

IV. Philip Seeks To Bring Others To Christ:

Read: *John 12:20–24*

A. *A Possible Problem*:

Certain Greeks approached Philip (Philip is a Greek name) desiring to meet the Lord Jesus Christ–*verse 21*
The problem was that the Lord's ministry was directed to the *"lost sheep of the house of Israel"* (*Matthew 10:6; 15:24.*)
1. Philip's Desire–to bring men to Christ
2. Philip's Concern–would Jesus receive them?

B. *A Practical Solution*:

Philip went and told Andrew, then
went with him to see Jesus.
1. Strength in Numbers–*Ecclesiastes 4:9*
2. Andrew was closer to the Inner Circle
There will *always* be obstacles and difficulties when winning others to Christ, *II Corinthians 4:3, 4; Acts 13:8*. Here we observe the value of innovation. Where there's a will, there's a way! *See: Mark 2:-5.*

V. Philip Learns The "Fullness Of The Godhead Bodily":

Read: *John 14:7–11; Colossians 2:8–10*

Practical, analytical Philip was still seeking more evidence. Christ's answer was:

"He that hath seen me hath seen the Father"—a clear, direct statement of His deity *(verse 9)*. Jesus directed Philip to:

    A. *His Words—verse 10*
    B. *His Works—verse 11*

> It is now time to *believe*, not figure!—*verse 12*. Again we see the necessary balance between practical reasoning and belief. *Colossians 2:8* warns against philosophy and vain deceit—i.e. examining the Word of God at the bar of human reason. That's deadly! It also warns against tradition and rudiments (usually things which are observable, tangible, or do-able.) These too are vain (empty)—*Matthew 15:3, 6, 9*. Like Philip, we also must learn that yes, there is a place for a practical and analytical approach to the Christian life, but ultimately that life must rest fully in Jesus Christ and upon His Word. That's *faith*!

THE APPLICATION:

Philip's practical and analytical nature addresses a vital issue—that of our relationship and response to the authority of the Word of God. There are *two* things to avoid:

An unquestioning "faith"—blindly believing what we are told. The Scriptures are to be studied *(II Timothy 2:15)*, searched *(John 5:39)*, and compared *(I Corinthians 2:13d.)*.

A questioning "faith"—continuing to seek 'proofs' and reasons after God has clearly spoken *(II Timothy 3:7)*. The Bible is not meant to be debated, it's meant to be believed.

THE LESSON:

    A. *Relate the Story of Philip*
        1. Use a map to show where he lived.
        2. Tell the story of how Jesus called him to be a disciple—*John 1:43*
        3. Relate how Philip was a blessing to others—in the feeding of the 5,000 and bringing the Greeks to Jesus. When teaching children, use visual aids—pictures, flannel graph, etc.

    B. *Teach the Quality of Practical Faith*
        1. Show that we are to *search* the Scriptures

2. Show that we are to *submit* to the Scriptures
Use the illustration of a child's relationship to its parents. When the child is young he must learn to obey without reason or explanation. As the child matures, a wise parent will take time to explain the "why." The child must still obey, of course.

C. *Conclude With the lesson On True Faith*
1. Teach and explain the memory verse.
2. Review the names of the twelve apostles.

DISCUSSION:

- How does *Isaiah 55:8,9* enter into the lesson learned from the character of the apostle Philip?

- List some things God asks us to do that are not "reasonable" from a human perspective.

- List some amazing miracles God has done in and through our Church in the field of our evangelistic endeavor.

- What are some practical ways we can "check out the preacher" (in the spirit of *Acts 17:11*) when listening to a sermon?

- In *Matthew 15:32–38*, the Lord performed a second miracle of feeding a great multitude.

- Although Philip is not mentioned by name, what lessons in faith (if any) do you think the disciples learned from the first such miracle recorded in *John 6*? How does *Mark 6:51, 52* address this?

Philip

Sermon Title: The Real Doubting Disciple

Text: John 1:43

Before we can change the world, we've got to let God change us. That's what the Christian life is all about. It's about letting Him mold you and make you into the person He wants you to be. It's about walking and talking with Jesus like these men did, because as you spend time with Jesus, you'll soon discover that you are becoming more and more like him. The Bible says in *Romans 8:9* that once we're saved (That's redemption), we are predestined to be conformed to the image and likeness of Jesus (That's sanctification). And then the Bible says in *Philippians 3:21* that one day God will *"transform our lowly body that it may be conformed to His glorious body"* (That's glorification).

Change is a main characteristic of the Christian life. It's a total transformation from the old selfish, sinful man to the new perfected person that Jesus desires for you to be. It begins the moment you say "yes" and follow Jesus, but it isn't complete until you reach heaven and receive your glorified body.

It is my prayer that this is what you're learning as we look at the different disciples. These were just ordinary, average, run of the mill men, who became extraordinary because of their closeness and relationship with Jesus.

Now, some of the transformations took place rather quickly, as in the case of Andrew or John. Some of the transformations took a little longer, as in the case of Peter or James. But then there are those transformations that you look at, but they never seem to quite get there–like in the case of today's disciple, a man by the name of Philip.

So, what do we know about this man named Philip? Well, fortunately we know more about him than say, Matthew or Thomas, but unfortunately, not as much as Peter or John.

He had a Greek name which means "lover of horses." He had a Greek name, but we know that all the disciples were Jews. He was what was known as a "Hellenist." That means that his family was Jewish, but they had adopted the Greek language, Greek culture, and Greek customs.

He was from Bethsaida, the same town as Andrew and Peter. Most likely he was another of the "fishermen disciples." And then, as you encounter him in the pages of the Bible, you find that Philip was a facts and figures guy. He was a by the book, practical, non-forward thinking kind of a man. John MacArthur even calls him "the bean counter." He's a man who's more comfortable with the pages of the apostle's policy manual than he was with the people that the apostles encountered. He couldn't see the forest for the trees. He had a tendency to be a pragmatist and pessimist. And really, like I entitled this message, Philip was the real doubting disciple, because as you read about him in three out of the four main sections of Scripture that deal with Philip, he's usually telling you why it can't be done, rather than looking to Jesus to see the impossible become a miracle.

I am trying to point out both the strengths and the weaknesses of these disciples as I do this study. We're going to see them as they experience the thrill of victory as well as the agony of defeat.

Now, everything that we know about the personality of Philip comes from the gospel of John. Matthew, Mark, and Luke give us absolutely no details of his life. They simply put him in the list with the other disciples. All of the pictures of his personality come from John's gospel, so let's just journey through the gospel of John and delve into the life of a disciple by the name of Philip.

Here's the first thing that I want you to see.

His Divine Encounter

I begin in *John 1:43, "The following day Jesus wanted to go to Galilee, and He found Philip and said to him, Follow Me. Now Philip was from Bethsaida, the city of Andrew and Peter. Philip found Nathanael and said to him, We have found Him of whom Moses in the law, and also the prophets, wrote; Jesus of Nazareth, the son of Joseph."*

This presents us with what is really one of the greatest tensions in the entire Bible. John made it a point to say that Jesus wanted to go to Galilee to find Philip. It states that Jesus went to Galilee for the specific purpose of finding and calling Philip. He's the first one that Jesus physically sought out and the first one to whom Jesus actually said, "Follow Me."

Do you remember what Philip said when he went running to tell Nathanael? *"We have found Him."* Do you see the tension? Do you sense the struggle that some people have with this whole matter of whether God chooses us or we choose God? People have struggled with that question for thousands of years. Theologians have debated that question since the days that Jesus physically walked on this earth. There have been those who have actually fought and been killed over this so-called debate between the doctrine of sovereign election and the free-will of man. And here it is, really presented in the course of just a few words—*"Jesus found Philip"* and *"We have found Him."*

Do you want to know the answer to the question of "Does God choose us or do we choose God?" The answer is "yes." God did choose us. The Bible says that God *loved us before we ever loved Him*. The Bible says that *Jesus came to seek and to save that which was lost*. But is also says that we are to *seek the Lord while He may be found, and call upon Him while He is near*. The Bible says, "*You will seek Me and find Me, when you search for Me with all your heart.*" It says that *whosoever will call upon the Lord will be saved*. Do you want to know who the "elect" are? They are the "whosoever wills!"

Somebody once asked Billy Sunday what he thought about this whole matter of sovereign election and the free-will of man. He said, "I believe that when I get to heaven, as I walk up to the pearly gates, there will be a sign that says, *"Whosoever will may come."* And then as I walk through those glimmering gates and look back I'll see another sign that says, "*Predestined from the foundation of the world.*"

You see, theologically we'll never be able to fully and finally grasp the greatness of God's glorious salvation. Anybody who says that they do is either not being ethical or logical because there's no way that our finite mind could completely comprehend the heart and mind of the infinite God.

Jesus was searching for Philip and Philip was searching for Jesus. Philip said, *"We have found Him of whom Moses in the law, and also the prophets, wrote..."* Why would he say that? Because he'd been searching for Jesus his entire life. When he grew up going to synagogue with Peter and Andrew, they had heard about the Messiah. They had read about the One who would be born of the house and the lineage of David. They had dreamed about the day that the Messiah would come to set them free.

They had sung the songs that said that the deliverer was coming. Philip had been looking and waiting and watching for the Messiah for all of his life.

Philip was looking for Jesus and Jesus was looking for Philip. Let me give you the greatest news that anybody could ever give you–just like Jesus personally went to Galilee to call and convert Philip, Jesus personally came to this world to seek and to save you.

His Doubtful Expression

Now, let's look in *John 6*. This is the second scene that gives us a glimpse into the personality of Philip. It's the so-called "feeding of the five thousand," and I call it the "so-called" feeding of the five thousand because five thousand was just the number of men that were there. Most Bible scholars say that we're probably talking about 15,000 to 20,000 people sitting on that mountainside waiting for a meal. But in verse 5, John records a conversation between Jesus and Philip. *"Then Jesus lifted up His eyes, and seeing a great multitude coming toward Him, He said to Philip, "Where shall we buy bread, that these may eat?"* (Now, why did Jesus single Philip out? John tells us...) *but this He said to test him, for He Himself knew what He would do."* You see, evidently Philip was the apostolic administrator. Again, like John MacArthur says, he was "the bean counter."

Now, as we study these disciples, what you're going to see is that they all seem to have had their assigned roles and responsibilities within Jesus's group of 12. We know that Judas was in charge of keeping the money. Peter seems to have been the guy in charge of transportation. It makes sense that someone else was in charge of making arrangements both for food and for lodging. And evidently that person was Philip, because he seems to have been the one who was most concerned with organization and administration. And by the way, it fit his personality.

So, Jesus comes to Philip, knowing his personality. Jesus knew he would add up all of the people and multiply the meals and he says, *"Philip answered Him, Two hundred denarii's worth of bread is not sufficient for them, that every one of them may have a little."*

Jesus tested Philip and Philip failed the test big time. Philip should have looked at the crowd and said, "Lord, I've been doing some figuring in my head, and I don't think that we have enough to feed them by ourselves, but since you're the Bread of Life, I know You can." Instead,

Philip says, "It looks impossible to me." Hey, can I tell you something? We serve a God who specializes in the impossible. It may seem like you are faced with an impossible situation - your marriage is on the rocks, your family is in ruins, your job situation is in jeopardy, you've just gotten a bad report from the doctor and a good outcome seems impossible–listen, with God nothing is impossible. The Bible says that in *Mark 10:27*.

The impossible doesn't take Jesus any extra time at all. He specializes in the impossible. Philip should have known that. He's seen Jesus turn the water into wine at the wedding feast of Cana. He'd just seen Jesus heal a man who'd been paralyzed for 38 years. I mean, you talk about impossible; Jesus specializes in making the impossible, not just possible, but a reality. Philip should have known that.

But now, go back to our text. In verse 6 John says that the reason why Jesus asked Philip this question was to test him. In your life there will be times when you will face tests from the Lord and temptations from the devil. So, how can you tell the difference? Here's how. When Jesus tests you He does so to make you better. When Satan tempts you, he does so to make you fall. When Jesus tests you, He wants to reveal something to you; when the devil tempts you, he wants to ruin you.

You see, Jesus already knew what He was going to do. He knew that there was a little boy there who had some loaves and fishes. He knew that He was going to multiply them and feed them to those thousands of people and that there were gong to be 12 baskets full of leftovers. Jesus knew all of that. What He wanted was for Philip to see things from Heaven's point of view, rather than from an earthly point of view. Philip had faith, but evidently it was a weak and a worldly faith, and what Jesus wanted him to put aside all of his materialistic, pragmatic, common-sense solutions and lay hold of the supernatural power that comes from a rock-ribbed faith in the living Lord Jesus Himself.

His Disappointing Exclamation

Let's look now at *John 14*. This is one of my favorite passages in the entire Bible. Jesus had just enjoyed his last supper with His disciples. He's told them that He's going to have to leave them. He's even told them that one of them would betray Him and another would deny Him. But then in *John 14:1* Jesus begins to give them the secrets of an untroubled heart. *"Let not your heart be troubled; you believe in God, believe also in Me. In My Father's house are many mansions; if it were not so, I would have told you. I go to prepare a place for you. And if I go and prepare a place for you, I will come again and receive you to Myself; that where I am, there you may be also. And where I go you know, and the way you know." Thomas said to Him, "Lord, we do not know where You are going, and how can we know the way?" Jesus said to him, "I am the Way, the Truth, and the Life. No one comes to the Father except through Me. If you had known Me, you would have known My Father also; and from now on you know Him and have seen Him." Philip said to Him, "Lord, show us the Father, and it is sufficient for us."*

Every time I read that statement it absolutely astounds me. I just don't understand how Philip didn't get what Jesus had just said. Jesus had just told his disciples, really in the plainest possible sense that He and the Father were of the same essence. Jesus was the way to the Father, the truth about the Father, and the life from the Father. The only sight of the Father was in the face of Jesus, and Philip had been looking upon that face for almost three years, and he still didn't get it. He had followed Jesus and worked for Jesus and been taught by Jesus. He had been privileged to witness and preach and perform miracles in Jesus's name, but here when Jesus is spending His last moments with these men, Philip missed it.

Jesus responded graciously by saying, *"Have I been with you so long, and yet you have not known Me, Philip? He who has seen Me has seen the Father; so how can you say, 'Show us the Father?' Do you not believe that I am in the Father, and the Father in Me? The words that I speak to you I do not speak on My own authority; but the Father who dwells in Me does the works. Believe Me that I am in the Father and the Father in Me, or else believe Me for the sake of the works themselves."*

Let's be reminded by this that Jesus is the visible expression of God the Father. If you want a picture of the Heavenly Father, then study and get to know the Son.

Whatever you are facing in your life today, would you turn that over to Jesus and trust Him with it? He is the One who sought you, called you, and loves you.

MATTHEW

The Publican turned Preacher

LESSON TEXT:

Luke 5:27–32

STUDY TEXTS:

Matthew 9:9–13; Matthew 10:3, Mark 2:14 17; Mark 3:18; Luke 5:27–32; Luke 6:15; Acts 1:13

MEMORY VERSE:

Luke 5:32–"I came not to call the righteous, but sinners to repentance."

THE STUDY:

I. The Publican's Circumstances:
　A. *His Name*:
　　1. *Matthew*–from Mattathias, *"a gift of the Lord."*
　　2. *Levi (his surname)–Luke 5:27*
　　This may indicate his tribal name. If so, the Levites were the priestly tribe and as such were not given a portion of the Promised Land (*Deuteronomy 10:8, 9.*) They were supposed to collect tithes, not taxes (*Hebrews 7:5).*
　　3. *The Son of Alphaeus–Mark 2:14*
　　This could mean he was the brother of the apostle James the Less (*Luke 6:15)*, although this is not conclusive.
　B. *His Location*:
　　Matthew dwelt in (or near) the city of Capernaum–Mark 2:1, 13, 14
　　1. It was where the Lord Jesus lived–*Matthew 4:13*
　　2. It was a center of taxation–*Matthew 7:24* (no doubt because of its fishing industry). The highway from Damascus to the Mediterranean passed through it.
　　3. It was an unrepentant city–*Matthew 8:5–13, 7:24–27; Mark 1:21–34; 2:1–12; John 4:46–54*

C. *His Station*:

From *Luke 5:29* it would appear that Matthew was a man of some wealth. Compare this with *Luke 19:2*

II. The Publican's Character:

A. *What Is A "Publican?"*

1. The title comes from the Latin (Roman) *"publicannus"*– literally: a "public servant," a government employee.

2. Publicans were contracted by the Romans as tax collectors–*Luke 5:27*

3. Most publicans *were* corrupt. They lined their own pockets by collecting more taxes and duties than required. They did this though:

   a. Overcharging–*Luke 3:13*

   b. Extortion by false accusation–*Luke 9:8d*

   The Romans permitted their extortion so long as it did not lead to public insurrection.

4. Publicans were usually wealthy men–*Luke 5:29; 19:2*

B. *What People Thought of Publicans*

Publicans were considered to be piranhas within Jewish society. They were classified along with the worst of sinners–*Matthew 9:11; 11:19; Luke 18:11*

The strict Jews resented the tax collectors with a passion. They believed only the Lord should receive their tribute. Publicans were barred from being a witness or a judge, and were kept from worshipping at the temple (The publican in *Luke 18* stood *afar off*).

C. *What About Paying Taxes?*

1. Christians are to pay their taxes–*Romans 13:6, 7*

2. Christ paid the taxes imposed upon Him–*Matthew 17:24–27; Luke 20:22–25*

III. The Publican's Conversion:

Like all the apostles, Matthew was saved then baptized under the ministry of John the Baptist. The actual account of Matthew's salvation would fit in with *Luke 3:3–14*. John preached repentance (*Luke 3:8*) and faith (*John 1:29*), the same Gospel message we preach today.

In *Luke 3:12* we read that publicans came to John presenting themselves for baptism (indicating they had exercised faith in Christ). The evidence of genuine conversion John sought was *not* that they quit being tax collectors, but that they quit being *crooked* tax collectors, *Luke 3:13*. It is reasonable to assume that Matthew *was* one of those publicans. Imagine his testimony in Capernaum–an honest tax collector!

There are some tremendous truths to be learned here:

    A. *Christ Came to Save Lost Sinners*
        Luke 19:10; I Timothy 1:15
    B. *Christ Receiveth Sinful Men*
        Luke 15:1; 19:2–10
    C. *The Vilest Offender Who Truly Believes…*
        That moment from Jesus a pardon receives! *Luke 18:9–14*
    D. *Repentance & Faith in Christ Saves ANY Man*
        Matthew 21:31, 32; Luke 7:29, 30; Hebrews 7:25

The Pharisees shut themselves out of the kingdom of God through their prideful self-righteousness–*Matthew 23:13*

The only person Christ cannot save is one who willfully rejects His gracious invitation to be saved–*Romans 2:1–6; Hebrews 10:26, 27, 38, 39; II Thessalonians 2:10–12*

IV. The Publican's Call:

Matthew 9:9–13; Mark 2:14–17 and *Luke 5:27–32* record the call of Matthew Levi into "full time Christian service."

When Christ called him:

    A. *He Left All*
        Luke 5:28. This is the attitude of true discipleship–*Luke 14:33*. Lordship demands it! Notice his response was immediate. He was giving up a life of great wealth, but it meant nothing to him. *cf. Philippians 3:7, 8*
    B. *He Rose Up*
        Luke 5:28. Discipleship is a life of action
    C. *He Followed*
        Luke 5:28. This defines discipleship *Matthew 4:19; 16:24; John 1:43; 12:26*
    D. *He Celebrated*
        Luke 5:29. Perhaps this was a farewell feast. Maybe, like Elisha in *I Kings 19:19–21*, Matthew was "burning his bridges." Certainly, he sought to reach his own crowd. He wanted them to receive what he had found in Christ. Christ was his honored guest!

The disciple Matthew later became the apostle Matthew. We read nothing further of him in the Scriptures after Acts 1:13. Of course, as tradition universally affirms, Matthew also was the human writer of the Gospel which bears his name–the Gospel which presents Jesus Christ as the *king*. Legend has Matthew preaching in Judea, before taking the Gospel to heathen lands (possibly Ethiopia) where he was martyred.

THE APPLICATION:

There are *three* important lessons to learn from the story of Matthew:

- Christ is able to save anyone who comes to Him in faith
- Christ is able to use anyone, despite their past
- Obedience to the claims and call of Christ needs to be instant and thorough

THE LESSON:

A. *Relate the Story of Matthew*
   1. Use a map to show where he lived
   2. Be sure to explain what he was and what he did
   3. Tell how Jesus Christ came to save sinners
   When teaching children, use visual
   aids–pictures, flannel graph, etc.

B. *Teach the Qualities of True Discipleship*
   1. Instant submission and obedience to Christ
   2. Understanding true value–*I Timothy 6:17–19*
   3. Remembering to reach those from whence
   we came–family, friends, work mates, etc.

DISCUSSION:

Consider the story of Matthew together with *Luke 14:21–24* in light of our Church's outreach program. Who still needs reaching in our community? Plan a 'specialized' Gospel presentation you might give to someone who is considered by society to be a wicked person–drunks, drug addicts, etc. Make a list of men and women God has used despite their wicked past (Bible, historic, and more recent examples).

Matthew

Title: The Tax Collector's Change

Text: Luke 5:27–32 / Luke 15

We come to the one who is perhaps the least likely of all the men to have been chosen and changed by Jesus–a tax collector by the name of Matthew.

Now, of course, there are a lot of things that we could say about taxes and tax collectors. I like what one commentator said, "There is one big difference between death and taxes–death doesn't get worse every time congress meets." You know, if it weren't so serious, it would be funny, but this country was originally founded as a protest against taxation. As one writer put it, "Our founding fathers objected to taxation without representation. They should see it now with representation."

I heard about a man who got the call to come in for a complete audit. After a couple of hours of going over his papers, the IRS agent said, "You know, I really have to question some of the deductions that you've put down here." "Like what?" the guy said. "Well, let's begin with where you claimed depreciation on your wife."

Well, Matthew may have laughed at that, but he certainly wouldn't have liked it and he definitely wouldn't have allowed it. So, let's look there in *Luke 5:27* and let me share with you "The Tax Collector's Change."

Luke 5:27–32, "After these things He went out and saw a tax collector named Levi (That's Matthew's other name), sitting at the tax office. And He said to him, "Follow Me." So he left all, rose up, and followed Him. Then Levi gave Him a great feast in his own house. And there were a great number of tax collectors and others who sat down with them. And their scribes and the Pharisees complained against His disciples, saying, why do you eat and drink with tax collectors and sinners? Jesus answered and said to them, those who are well have no need of a physician, but those who are sick. I have not come to call the righteous, but sinners, to repentance."

Here we are told about the conversion of a crook. This is the story of Matthew, the terrible tax collector, who became one of Jesus's 12 trusted disciples. This may come as a shock to you, but when Jesus called Matthew to forsake all and follow Him, not everybody liked it. The Pharisees and the scribes, the religious crowd of that day, were amazed and appalled. There was no single group of people in that day that were more hated, more despised and more detested than the Jewish tax collectors. They were evil men who were using their position to become wealthy at the expense of everybody else around them.

Palestine was a province of Rome and it was being crushed under the heel of Rome. And greedy Rome needed more and more money to feed its expanding empire and to grease its wicked war machine. They were collecting taxes on everything. Rome would set a certain amount of money that had to be raised, and everything that the tax collectors could raise above that they were able to keep.

As a result, the people of this day looked upon them as crooks and traitors. You can imagine how they hated these tax collectors. As a matter of fact, a tax collector couldn't be a judge, he couldn't be a witness, and he couldn't even go into the synagogue to pray. Do you remember over in *Luke 18*, the Bible talks about the Pharisee and the tax collector who went into the synagogue to pray? Do you remember what it says? It says that the tax collector *"stood afar off."* People treated them like they had the plague; like they had leprosy. They hated them. They detested them. They despised them.

Now, the Bible says that when Jesus called Matthew, that Matthew just got up and left everything that he had and followed Jesus. And not only did he follow Jesus, but he did something that sent all of the religious folks of that day into orbit. He put on a banquet in Jesus's honor and invited all of his friends—and you know what kind of friends he would have had—all of the tax collectors and all of the sinners and all of the outcasts of society and there was Jesus sitting and eating in the middle of them. The Pharisees started to complain and criticize and condemn Him by saying, *"How in the world can you, the One who claims to be the Messiah, spend time with sinful, perverted people like this?"* And in response to that critical question, Jesus made one of the greatest, most grace-filled statements in the entire Bible. He said, *"Those who are well have no need of a physician, but those who are sick. I have not come to call the righteous, but sinners, to repentance."*

Well, that didn't help the situation at all. It was like pouring gas on a fire. Look in *Luke 15:1*, *"Then all the tax collectors and the sinners drew near to Him to hear Him."* You see, when Jesus saved Matthew, He started a movement. The news got out that *"this man is a friend of sinners."* And so, now, not only is Matthew following Jesus, but so are the folks that Matthew invited to the dinner. That's why verse 1 says that *"all the tax collectors and the sinners drew near to Him to hear Him. But, the Pharisees and scribes complained, saying, This Man receives sinners and eats with them."* By the way, aren't you glad that Jesus receives sinners?

I Timothy 1:15, *"This is a faithful saying and worthy of all acceptance, that Christ Jesus came into the world to save sinners..."*

The tax collectors and the sinners were following and listening to Jesus. The Pharisees and the scribes were verbally criticizing and condemning Jesus for keeping company with people like Matthew and his crowd, the tax collectors and sinners.

That's why Jesus gave this one parable in *Luke 15*. It was given in order to answer the question of why Jesus ate with tax collectors and kept company with sinners. It should help us understand why Jesus chose and changed a tax collector by the name of Matthew into one of His 12 disciples.

Man's Terrible Problem

You see, this parable tells us about the nature of men. He says that we're weak, like a lost sheep. Look in verse 4, *"What man of you, having a hundred sheep, if he loses one of them, does not leave the ninety-nine in the wilderness, and go after the one which is lost until he finds it? And when he has found it, he lays it on his shoulders, rejoicing. And when he comes home, he calls together his friends and neighbors, saying to them, Rejoice with me, for I have found my sheep which was lost!"*

Now, don't get the idea that Jesus is paying us a compliment by calling us sheep. You see, sheep are dumb and directionless. I mean, if a sheep gets to eating and the shepherd doesn't keep an eye on it, it will just wander off and get lost. It doesn't have any sense of direction. A horse can come back home. A dog can come back home. A cat can come back home. A bird can come back home, but not a sheep. He just keeps on going. He'll nibble a little bit here and he'll nibble a little bit there and before he knows it, he's wandered off and he doesn't know how to get back. That's why the Bible says in *Isaiah 53*, *"All we like sheep have gone astray..."*

Sheep are also defenseless. You know, just about every other animal has some sort of ability of fight or flight. A rabbit can run. A dog can bite. A cat can scratch. God seems to have equipped most animals with some sort of method of defense, but what can a sheep do? It can't run. It can't fight. It's totally and completely defenseless. Jesus in essence was saying, "You want to know why I keep company with people like Matthew? I'll tell you why. They're so weak. They're so dumb. They're so defenseless. They have no sense of direction. If I don't help them, nobody will."

Man's Worthlessness

You see, when Jesus told this story, he didn't just point out the fact that a man like Matthew was weak like a lost sheep, He also pointed out the fact that a man like Matthew was worthless like a lost coin. Look in verse 8, *"Or what woman, having ten silver coins, if she loses one coin, does not light a lamp, sweep the house, and search carefully until she finds it? And when she has found it, she calls her friends and neighbors together, saying, "Rejoice with me, for I have found the piece which I lost!"*

There's nothing weaker than a lost sheep, and there's nothing more worthless than a lost coin. You see, a coin is supposed to be saved, spent or invested, but it's not supposed to be lost. When God created Matthew, He had a plan for him. God wanted to treasure Matthew. God wanted to use Matthew. He wanted to invest in Matthew. Matthew was God's creation. But when Matthew was lost, he wasn't doing the thing that God created him to do. That's what the Bible is talking about in *Romans 3:12* where it says, *"They have all turned aside; They have together become unprofitable."* You see, Matthew wasn't supposed to be making a profit for Rome. Matthew wasn't even supposed to be making a profit for Matthew. Matthew was supposed to be making profit for the Lord.

By the way, God had a purpose when He made you. God had a plan when He made you. God had a design and a desire when He made you and until you do what God wants you to do; you're worthless like a lost coin.

The devil's plan was to make Matthew's life a disgrace to God. That was the devil's plan. He wanted to have Matthew's life lost in dirt, lost in darkness and lost in disgrace.

Man's Wretchedness

In verse 11 and following is a story of a wayward, wicked, and worldly son. Here's the story of a weeping, waiting and willing father. It's the story of the prodigal son. This young man had sown the seeds of sin and as a result he had reaped the fruit of sin. You say, "What kind of fruit did he reap?"

He reaped the fruit of pleasure. The Bible says that "*he wasted his possessions with prodigal living.*" He had a ball. He had a wonderful time. You say "Wait a minute, pastor; don't tell these young people that sin is fun." I'd be a fool if I didn't, because even the Bible talks about the pleasures of sin. Now, it's not the joy of sin, it's the pleasure of sin, and there's a big difference, but even the pleasures of sin only last for a season. The devil's too smart to go fishing without any bait. He wouldn't get anybody to sin if there weren't some amount of sensual pleasure in sin.

I heard about a man one day who was seen walking along with a basket of beans on his arm, dropping little handfuls of those beans on the ground and behind him was a bunch of pigs, all lined up, walking behind that man and eating those little handfuls of beans. Somebody said, "What are you doing? Isn't that a weird way to feed pigs?" He said, "I'm not feeding them, this is how I take them to the slaughter house."

Satan has a basket on his arm, and in that basket are what we call the pleasures of sin, and so many people are following along, just like this prodigal son, right into the devil's slaughter house.

Then he tasted poverty. "*He began to be in want.*" The Bible says, "*Bread gained by deceit is sweet to a man, But afterward his mouth will be frilled with gravel.*" You see, you have to get the whole picture. You have to see it from beginning to end to really understand how much sin costs. It costs character. It costs influence. It costs reputation. It costs time. It costs wealth. It costs love. It costs home. It will cost you your soul. And it will cost you heaven itself. It costs to serve Satan, it costs everyday. It costs every step of the way.

If you think that you can sin and get away with you, you're wrong. If you think that God has canceled His law that says that the wages of sin is death, you're wrong. The Bible says, "*The soul that sins, it will surely die.*" The Bible says, "*Be sure your sins will find you out.*"

It also cost this young man slavery. The Bible says that *he went and joined himself to a citizen of that country and he was sent into the field to feed swine*. That's where he was, out there living and eating with the pigs, when he could have been home in his father's house eating like a prince.

Jesus is showing how sin will cost you and where sin will take you. He's saying, "The reason why I spend time with Matthew and keep company with sinners is because they're impoverished and imprisoned by sin like this lost son, and they need me."

God's Tremendous Purpose

You see, Jesus didn't just give this parable to teach us about the nature of man, He also gave this parable to teach us about the nature of God. And since we serve and love a triune God–God the Father, God the Son and God the Holy Spirit–there are three parts of this parable that are given to teach us the purpose of God in saving sinful man.

A. The rescuing purpose of the Son. *Luke 15:4*

What man of you, having an hundred sheep, if he loses one of them, doth not leave the ninety and nine in the wilderness, and go after that which is lost, until he find it? The shepherd who went after the lost sheep is a picture of the Lord Jesus Christ, the Son of God, who was sent into the world to rescue us. Jesus said, *"I am the Way, the Truth and the Life, no man comes to the Father except by me." "I am the good shepherd who lays down His life for His sheep."*

B. The revealing purpose of the Spirit. *Luke 15:8*

Either what woman having ten pieces of silver, if she lose one piece, doth not light a candle, and sweep the house, and see diligently till she find it?

Who does the woman who lit that lamp and swept that house represent? She represents the revealing purpose of the Holy Spirit of God. When we're down in the dirt and the darkness and disgrace of sin, it's the Holy Spirit who turns on the light and stirs up the dust in order to reveal and convict us of our sin. Aren't you glad that God sent His Holy Spirit into this world? You're not supposed to be sitting around in darkness and dirt and disgrace. God loves you and the same God who took a tax-collecting crook like Matthew and made him an apostle is the same God who can take you and do something wonderful with your life.

C. The receiving purpose of the Father. *Luke 15:20*

And he arose, and came to his father. But when he was yet a great way off, his father saw him, and had compassion, and ran, and fell on his neck, and kissed him.

The father in this parable represents God the Father. Can't you just see it? Here's the old father sitting on the front porch. The years have come and gone. He's looked down that long road on which that boy left so many times. Not a day has gone by which He hasn't gone out to wait for his boy to come home. He's sitting there rocking on that front porch and he looks down the road and there he sees a figure walking toward the house. The father's heart knows that it's his boy, and Jesus says that *even when he was a great way off, the father saw him*. That means that he was looking for him. And then get this–the Bible says that *he ran to meet him*. He ran! Can't you see that old man as he holds that robe in his hand and runs out to meet that boy! Can't you see him as he throws open his arms and wraps them around that boy in a big old bear hug? Can't you see him as he tells them to put new sandals on his feet and kill the fatted calf and throw a party! His boy who was lost is found.

That's what God's trying to tell us in this story–He's waiting like a father to receive you. I don't care what you've done. I don't care where you've been. I don't care how deep in sin you've gone, God says, "I love you, come home." That's the reason Jesus kept company with people like Matthew. He wanted to rescue them and receive them in order to fulfill His purpose for their lives.

JUDAS ISCARIOT

The Betrayer of Christ

LESSON TEXT:

Matthew 26:14–16, 20–25, 47–50

STUDY TEXTS:

Matthew 10:4; Matthew 27:3–10; Mark 3:19; Mark 14:10, 11, 43–46; Luke 6:16; Luke 22:3–6, 21–23, 47, 48; John 6:70, 71; John 12:1–6; John 13:2, 18–30; John 18:1–5; Acts 1:16–20, 25

MEMORY VERSE:

Matthew 26:22–"And they were exceeding sorrowful, and began every one of them to say unto him, Lord, is it I?"

THE STUDY:

I. The Person Of Judas:
   A. *His Name*:
      1. Judas is the Greek form of the Hebrew "Judah," meaning "praise."
      2. There are *five* other men named Judas in the New Testament:
         a. Judas, the Lord's step-brother–*Matthew 13:55*
         b. Judas, not Iscariot–*John 14:22*. This was another named for the apostle Lebbeus Thaddeus. He is also called "the brother of James" (*Luke 6:16 and Acts 1:13*). It is likely he was the human writer of the epistle of Jude (*Jude 1.*)
         c. Judas of Galilee–*Acts 5:37*. This man was a Jewish insurrectionist.
           See: *Luke 13:1*
         d. Judas of Damascus–*Acts 9:11*. An unknown member of the church at Damascus who lived on Straight Street

e. Judas Barsabas–*Acts 15:22, 27, 32*. A leader and preacher prophet associated with the church at Jerusalem.

B. *His Background*

There are two pieces of information about the background of the apostle Judas Iscariot:

1. He was Simon's son–*John 6:71; 12:4; 13:2, 26.* This is an unknown Simon.
2. Iscariot is generally thought to mean "*man ('ish')* of *Kerioth.*" If this is the case, Judas would have come from the Judean village of Kerioth (*Joshua 15:25*) located south of Jerusalem. It would also mean that Judas was the only apostle who was not Galilean.

II. The Privilege Of Judas:

Read: *Acts 1:17*

A. *He was Numbered With The Twelve*

Although the Bible narrative is silent, we would assume that Judas Iscariot (like all the apostles) was baptized by John the Baptist. We *do* know that:

1. Jesus chose him–*Luke 6:13.* He did this *knowing* that Judas would betray Him (*John 6:70, 71*)
2. Many times over, Judas heard Christ teach and preach, saw His many miracles, and experienced first-hand His love and compassion–toward him (*John 13:1*) and toward the multitudes.
3. He had his feet washed by the Master–*John 13:4, 5*
4. At the final pre-Passover meal, Judas sat in a place of honor. As Christ, the apostles, and the other disciples gathered to eat, they would have reclined on low couches around the table–leaning on the left elbow and using the right hand to hold the food and drink. The apostle John, therefore, would have been on Christ's right (*John 13:23*). Judas must have been on His left, because the Lord was able to both dip the sop and give it to Judas.

NOTE: Judas departed *before* Jesus instituted the Lord's Supper–compare *John 13:30* with *Matthew 26:25, 26*

5. Even to the point of his betrayal of Christ, Jesus called him "friend"– *Matthew 26:50*
6. Ahithophels betrayal of David in *II Samuel 15–17* resulted in the penning of a Messianic prophecy in *Psalm 41:9* and *Psalm 55:12–14*. It shows the depth of the relationship between the Lord Jesus Christ and Judas Iscariot. Ahithophel is the "Judas Iscariot of the Old Testament"–*II Samuel 17:23*

B. *He Had a Ministry*

Like all the apostles:

1. He was given power–*Matthew 10:1*
2. He was sent to preach–*Matthew 10:5–7; Mark 3:14*
3. He was very active in ministry–*Mark 6:30, 31*

III. The Pretense Of Judas:

Judas is an example of *Matthew 7:21–23*. He was a lost preacher! The remarkable and sad thing is that in his case, Jesus *did* know him.

A. *Judas Was Trusted By All*

1. He was the first treasurer of the first church–*John 13:29*. This indicates he was considered honest and trustworthy.
2. When Christ announced He was to be betrayed, no one suspected Judas!
   a. Each asked, "Lord, is it I?"–*Matthew 26:21, 22*
   b. Even when Jesus gave them a clue, still no one thought it could be Judas– *Matthew 26:23; John 13:25, 26, 29*

B. *Judas's Heart Was Unregenerate*

In *John 12:4–6*, we are told that Judas was a thief. He was pilfering the Lord's money from the treasury of the Lord's church! See: *I Timothy 6:9, 10* He had profession without possession. In *John 13:10*, Jesus indicated that Judas had *never* been cleansed–"*ye are clean, but not all.*" In *John 17:12*, He said Judas was lost.

C. *Judas Iscariot and the Devil*

There is some interest as to whether Judas was a man or a devil. Consider what the Gospel of John has to say:
1. Judas is called a devil–*John 6:70*. However, this was in the sense that Peter was called Satan *(Matthew 16:23)*

2. The Devil put it in Judas's heart to betray Christ–*John 13:2*
3. Satan entered into Judas–*John 13:27*
4. Judas is called the "son of perdition"–*John 17:12*

We see here a progression in the way Satan used Judas to betray Christ.

IV. The Perfidy Of Judas:

Perfidy is the willful betrayal of fidelity, confidence, or trust. Judas Iscariot is forever known as the betrayer of our Lord

    A. *The Compact–Matthew 26:14–16*
        1. *Judas's Greed–"what will ye give me?"*
        2. *Judas's Price*–thirty pieces of silver.
        See: *Zechariah 11:12, 13*
    B. *The Kiss–Matthew 26:47–50*
        This took place around midnight in the Garden of Gethsemane.
        1. *The Mob*–Judas came with a great multitude of armed men. He led them to the place where he knew Jesus would be, *John 18:2.*
        2. *The Moment*–Judas said, *"Master, Master, Hail, Master"* and kissed Jesus. The fact that Judas had to identify Jesus in this fashion shows that our Lord was very average and Jewish in His physical appearance *(Isaiah 53:2)*. He was not some tall, long-haired, blue-eyed man with striking looks.
        3. *The Mayhem*
            a. The power of Christ revealed–*John 8:6*
            b. The purpose of Christ revealed–*John 18:10, 11*

V. The Penitence Of Judas:

If there was one thing that might be said in favor of Judas Iscariot, it could be that he may not have intended for Christ to be harmed. In Mark 14:44 he said to the soldiers, *"take him, and lead him away safely."*

    A. *Remorse, Not Repentance*–Matthew 27:3, 4.
        Judas was sorry when he found out what the chief priests and Jewish elders were going to do with Christ. However, his repentance (change of mind leading to a change of action) was misdirected–it was:

1. Toward himself–he was sorry for what his actions did to *him*.

2. Toward the chief priests and elders–for having abetted their wicked scheme.

3. *Not* toward God–*Acts 20:21; 26:20b; Hebrews 6:1*.

B. *Suicide, Not Salvation–Matthew 27:5; Acts 1:18, 19*

Putting together these two accounts of Judas's suicide, we can reconstruct what must have happened.

1. He hanged himself from a tree which overhung a precipice or drop of some distance

2. The rope subsequently broke causing the body (or the swollen, rotting corpse) of Judas to crash down and split open, disemboweling him. It was a tragic end to a tragic figure. Judas died *lost* forever (*John 17:12*). Death is always hopeless for a lost man—*Hebrews 9:27*.

VI. The Place Of Judas:

Acts 1:25c states that Judas went *"to his own place."* There is some prophetic speculation about this–based on the fact that Jesus referred to Judas as the "son of perdition" (*John 17:12*) as is the coming Antichrist (*II Thessalonians 2:3; Revelation 17:8, 11*). Will the Antichrist in fact be Judas Iscariot resurrected out of perdition? After all, the coming "Beast" will be energized by Satan (*Revelation 13:2d*) similar to Judas. Since the Antichrist will be an imitator of Christ, who better to do that (it is argued) than the man who spent time with Him–Judas Iscariot? Also, Judas *never* called Jesus "Lord." However, there really isn't anything significant about the word "perdition." The Greek word *apoleia* is elsewhere translated as 'destruction' and 'damnation,' and refers to the eternal destiny of all lost souls–*Philippians 1:28; Hebrews 10:39; II Peter 3:7*.

THE APPLICATION:

The important lesson to learn from the story of Judas is the necessity for a personal relationship with Christ through the new birth. Judas enjoyed a privileged relationship with Christ, but was not saved. Many today are:

- White-washed, but not blood-washed!
- On the Church's roll, but not on Heaven's roll.

- Reformed, but not Reborn.
- Confirmed, but not Converted.
- Professors, but not Possessors–*Titus 1:16*

"Examine yourselves, whether ye be in the faith; prove your own selves. Know ye not your own selves, how that Jesus Christ is in you, except ye be reprobates?" - *II Corinthians 13:5*

    A. *False Profession*
        1. Simon Magus–*Acts 8:5–13, 18–24*
        2. So Close, Yet So Far–*Mark 12:34; Acts 26:28*
        3. Baptism does not save–*Acts 19:3, 4*
        4. Devils can believe–*James 2:19*
        5. Tares look like wheat–*Matthew 13:24–30, 36–43*
    B. *True Possession–II Corinthians 5:17; II Timothy 2:19*
        1. *New* nature–*II Peter 1: 3, 4*
        2. *New* desire–*John 10:27; I John 2:3–6*
        3. *New* love–*Romans 5:5; I John 3:14; John 8:42; Philemon 5*
        4. *New* management–*Romans 8:14, 16; Galatians 5:16–18, 25; Romans 12:2*
        5. *New* understanding–*I Corinthians 2:14, 15; I John 2:20, 27; I John 5:20*

The Lesson:

    A. *Relate the Story of Judas Iscariot's Betrayal*
        1. Emphasize how he must have "come across" to the other disciples–*I Samuel 16:7*
        2. Explain that we do what we do because we are what we are–*Proverbs 23:7; Matthew 7:15–18* When teaching children, use visual aids–pictures, flannel graph, etc. Make up some bags with silver coins.
    B. *Challenge Those Who Are Old Enough To Examine Themselves*

Do not create unnecessary doubts by listing things you think ought to be present in a professing believer's life. The best way is to have the students compare themselves with God's Word. Let them form their own conclusions.

Discussion:

- Comment on this statement by Dr. Bob Jones, Sr.: *"Your reputation is what people think you are; your character is what you are."* Judas did not think to sell out Christ for money from day one. How did the sin of covetousness progress in his life to bring him to that point?

- Is it possible for Christians to "betray" their Lord and Saviour in some way?

- If so, how? What is Christ worth to you?

- Was Judas a free moral agent in his betrayal of Christ, or was he irresistibly compelled in some way to do it?

- What are some misconceptions about "repentance?"

Judas Iscariot

Sermon Title: The Tragedy of a Wasted Life

Matthew 26:47–49; 27:3–5

The most devilish defeat, the biggest betrayal, the wickedest waste of position and possibility ever was plotted and perpetrated by a devilish disciple by the name of Judas Iscariot. As a matter of fact, Judas is mentioned in every list of the twelve disciples, except the list that's found in Acts, and every single time that he's mentioned he's marked as either "the traitor" or "the one who betrayed Jesus." But perhaps the most accurate and applicable title ever given to this traitor by the name of Judas Iscariot was spoken by the One whom he betrayed in *John 17:12* where Jesus called him *"the son of perdition."* Do you know what the word *"perdition"* means? It means *"destruction"* or *"waste."* Here in *Matthew 26* we are told about the tragedy of a wasted life. Look at how Matthew recounts the situation and circumstance around the greatest betrayal in all of human history.

Matthew 26:47–49, "And while He was still speaking, behold, Judas, one of the twelve, with a great multitude with swords and clubs, came from the chief priests and elders of the people. Now His betrayer had given them a sign, saying, "Whomever I kiss, He is the One; seize Him." Immediately he went up to Jesus and said, "Greetings, Rabbi!" and kissed Him."

Do you know what Solomon said? He said that *"the wounds of a friend are faithful, but the kisses of an enemy are deceitful."*

Let me ask you a question: Have you ever been betrayed? Have you ever had someone whom you loved and trusted and confided in, turn on you and betray you? There is nothing that tears you apart like being betrayed by somebody you trusted. In Psalm 55 he talks about being betrayed by a close friend, one that he even went to the House of God with. But you trusted them and they turned on you. Nothing hurts like that, does it? I heard Charles Stanley say, "Once you've been betrayed, you never really get over it."

Judas committed the most colossal failure in all of human history.

He committed the most horrible, heinous act that anybody has ever committed. He betrayed the Lord Jesus; the pure, perfect, sinless, Holy Son of God. He sold Him out for a handful of money. And what did it get him? Well, look in…

Matthew 27:3–5, "Then Judas, His betrayer, seeing that He had been condemned, was remorseful and brought back the thirty pieces of silver to the chief priests and elders, saying, "I have sinned by betraying innocent blood." And they said, "What is that to us? You see to it!" Then he threw down the pieces of silver in the temple and departed, and went and hanged himself."

That's the tragedy and the treachery of a man by the name of Judas Iscariot. Now, there are two questions that I want to ask and answer in this message.

What Can We Learn About Judas Iscariot?

Judas is mentioned more times in the four Gospels than any of the other disciples. So, everybody's heard about him, but what can we learn about him?

He was a Judean. You Ask, "How do I know that?" Because of his name. The name "Judas" means "the Lord leads." That tells us a little about the hopes and dreams that his parents must have had for him when he was born. But the sad fact is that there has never been a person that was more clearly led by Satan than Judas was.

During Jesus's day, the name "Judas" was one of the more popular and prominent names that parents gave to their baby boys. As a matter of fact, there are at least six men in the New Testament that were named Judas. It was a fine name. It was a blessed name. It was a special name, but because of one man's betrayal, nobody uses the name Judas today except on something like a goat. He turned a popular name into nothing more than a label reserved for the worst of traitors.

You say, "Yeah, but how do you know that he was a Judean?" Because of his second name. The name "Iscariot" means "man of Kerioth." Kerioth-hezron was a small town in the south of Judea. It wasn't much more than a wide spot in the road. Now, the thing that makes that so important is that Judas was the only disciple that wasn't from Galilee. Most of the other disciples were either friends or family. Judas was an outsider. That made it even easier for him to deceive the other disciples, because they didn't know anything about his family or his background or his life before he became a disciple.

He was religious. You say, "Of course he was, he was one of Jesus's disciples." That's right, but he was religious before he became a disciple. No doubt he was a good Jew. He wouldn't have wanted to be anything else. No doubt when he began to hear about this Rabbi from Galilee, who was going around healing people and raising people from the dead and preaching sermons that connected with people like never before, he wanted to be a part of that. So, like many of those other disciples, he followed Jesus and listened to him and learned from him. He even stayed behind when the crowds turned on Jesus and deserted Him in John 6. No doubt he made some sort of profession of faith and was even baptized. He preached with the other disciples. He ministered with the other disciples. He performed miracles like the other disciples. He did everything that the other disciples did. He was religious, but he was lost.

He was trusted. Did you know that Judas was the treasurer of the 12 disciples? He was the one that they trusted to hold the money. Now, I don't know about you, but to me that's a big deal. If I'm going to trust you to hold my money, I'm pretty much going to trust you with anything.

He was a hypocrite. The word "hypocrite" means "actor" or "pretender." In other words, they pretend to be something that they aren't. That's exactly what Judas was. He was a pretender. He was an actor. He was a hypocrite in the worst sense of the word.

Now, when or why his hypocrisy began, we don't know. Some believe that the devil made him do it. They believe that Satan somehow forced him to betray Jesus. Now, the Bible does say that it was the devil that put it into his heart to betray Jesus, but Satan couldn't make him, he couldn't coerce him, he couldn't force him. Judas acted of his own free will. He was responsible for selling the Son of God for the price of a slave.

Others believe that Judas was born to do what he did. That he had no choice. That he was predestined to play the part of the traitor. A.B. Bruce suggested that "Iscariot was chosen merely to be a traitor, as an actor might be chosen to play the part."

I totally reject that. That goes against everything that I know and believe about Jesus. I believe that Jesus chose each and every disciple with the purest of hearts and the most perfect of intentions, because otherwise that makes Jesus responsible for his own betrayal and Judas free from all blame.

Now, was Jesus deceived like those other disciples were about the nature and heart of Judas? No, not at all. He knew that Judas was greedy. He knew that Judas was power hungry. He knew that Judas was only going along with Him to further himself and his own goals. He knew that Judas was only following Him with his feet and not his faith. He knew that Judas's heart had never been changed. To be sure, nobody else did. Nobody else saw past the mask. Nobody else saw through to his heart. Who knows, maybe at the beginning, Judas himself didn't even know about it. The Bible says that *"the heart is desperately wicked and deceitful above all things, who can know it."* I'll tell you who, Jesus. The Bible says in Psalm 44 that he knows the secrets of the heart.

So, did Jesus know who was going to betray him? The Bible says that he did. In John 13, Jesus is washing the disciples' feet. Even Judas's feet. But then the Bible says something very interesting. In verse 11 it says that Jesus knew who would betray him; therefore he said, *"You are not all clean."* Here He is washing Judas's feet, fixing to go out and die for him, and Judas is still pretending to be one of His.

That's what we know about Judas. He was a Judean. He was religious. He was trusted. But most of all he was a hypocrite.

What Can We Learn From Judas Iscariot?

There's nothing that we can do for him. He's dead. He's in hell. Jesus even said that it would have been better if he had never been born. And by the way, that's true. If you die lost, it would have been better if you had never been born than to die on the wrong side of Jesus. But even though there's nothing that we can do for him, there are some lessons that we can learn from him.

A good beginning does not guarantee a godly ending. Go back to his name–Judas, "the Lord leads." Judas decided to follow Jesus. Judas heard Jesus teach. He went out two by two with the others, healing the sick and exorcising demons. Judas did a lot of disciple kinds of things. Yet he is not remembered for any of that. The only thing that we remember is how his relationship with Jesus ended. What does that teach us? How a life, a ministry, or a good relationship ends is absolutely crucial to everything that goes before it.

You can be close to Jesus and not be changed by Jesus. I can't get over the fact that here was a man who spent 24 hours a day with God in the flesh, Jesus Christ Himself. He watched Jesus eat, sleep, teach and preach. He saw Him heal people and raise people from the dead. No doubt Jesus would put His arm around him at times and talk to him. He was that close and yet he was so far away.

John MacArthur, "He had given his life to following Jesus, but he never gave Jesus his heart."

Maybe John Bunyan, who wrote *Pilgrim's Progress* had Judas in mind when he wrote, "Then I saw that there is a way to hell, even from the gates of Heaven."

You can act like a Christian and not be a Christian. There are many people who look like a Christian on the outside, but their heart has never really been changed. We can't always tell whether or not a person has genuinely been saved. The other disciples were fooled by Judas.

In the end, sin is no friend. Matthew tells us about what happened in chapter 27 when Judas came to his senses and realized what he had done. *"Then Judas, His betrayer, seeing that He had been condemned, was remorseful and brought back the thirty pieces of silver to the chief priests and elders, saying, "I have sinned by betraying innocent blood." And they said, "What is that to us? You see to it!" Then he threw down the pieces of silver in the temple and departed, and went and hanged himself."*

Judas thought that they were his friends. He thought that they would stand by him. He thought that they would accept him. He thought that they would understand, but in the end all that they did was use him to accomplish their ends and then turn their backs on him like he had on Jesus. So, he goes out and hangs himself and steps out into an eternity without Jesus.

That's the tragic story of a wasted life. Like Dr. Adrian Rogers put it, "That the story of a man who kissed the door of Heaven and went to hell."

LEBBAEUS THADDAEUS

Judas, not Iscariot

Lesson Text:

John 14:15–29

Study Texts:

Matthew 10:3; Mark 3:18; Luke 6:16; Acts 1:13; Jude 1

Memory Verse:

John 14:23–"Jesus answered and said unto him, If a man love me, he will keep my words: and my Father will love him, and we will come unto him, and make our abode with him."

The Study:

I. The Identity Of Judas:
    A. *His Family Name*:
        1. *Judas* is the Greek form of the Hebrew "Judah," meaning *"praise."*
        2. *Judas* was a common name in Israel. There are *five* other men so named in the New Testament:
            a. *Judas*, the step-brother of the Lord–*Matthew 13:55*
            b. *Judas* Iscariot–the betrayer of Christ–*Mark 14:10*
            c. *Judas* of Galilee–a Jewish insurrectionist–*Acts 5:37*
            d. *Judas* of Damascus–a member of the church at Damascus who lived on Straight Street–*Acts 9:11*
            e. *Judas* Barsabas–a preacher associated with the church at Jerusalem–*Acts 15:22 27, 32*
        3. Judas is called the "brother of James" in *Luke 6:16* and *Acts 1:13* (in proximity to James, the son of Alphaeus.)
            a. It is likely, though by no means certain, that Jude was the brother of the apostle James the Less.
            b. If this was the case, then there were three sets

of brothers numbered among the twelve–James
& John, Peter & Andrew, and James & Jude.
c. Some have identified this Judas to be the
half-brother of our Lord. However, up until
the resurrection, none of Christ's brothers
and sisters were believers–*John 7:5*.
B. *His Given Names*:
1. *Lebbaeus*–*"courageous"* (Derived from
the Hebrew *leb* = "heart")
2. *Thaddaeus*
Judas Lebbaeus Thattaeus has been called "trinomius"
(three-named.) This was not uncommon–See: *Acts 1:23*
C. *His Delineation*:

In *John 14:22* he is called "Judas, *not* Iscariot." Although his name was common, it must now have been associated with shame among the apostles. (Some have suggested that Judas had his name changed to *Lebbaeus Thaddaeus* in order to avoid this connection. However, he is called Judas in *Acts 1:13*–*after* the betrayal, after the resurrection.)

II. The Inquiry Of Judas:

The only recorded words of Judas are found in *John 14:22*–*"Lord, how is it that thou wilt manifest thyself unto us, and not unto the world?"*
A. *The Context*:
This exchange took place in the upper room–after Judas
Iscariot had left, after the institution of the Lord's
Supper, before the church sang a hymn and left for the
Garden of Gethsemane. In this discourse, Jesus spoke
to His disciples about His imminent death and return
to the Father. The apostles were full of questions:
Peter–*"Whither goest thou?"*–*John 13:36*
Thomas–*"How can we know the way?*–*John 14:5*
Philip–*"Shew us the Father"*–*John 14:8*
The Lord responded with words of encouragement
(*John 14:1–3)* and instruction (*John 13:34)*
B. *The Comfort*:
In answering Judas's question, Christ gave
three things by which He manifests Himself
to the believer and not to the world:

1. *He gave us His precepts* (Word)–*John 14:23a*
   See: *John 17:14, 17; I John 2:5*
Abiding in His Word brings assurance
2. *He gave us His abiding presence–John 14:23b*
John 14:16–26 and *John 16:7–14* outline the great promise of the Father to send the Comforter (the Holy Spirit) after the Lord Jesus Christ was glorified.
   a. Old Testament saints and New Testament believers (up until the sending of the Comforter in Acts 2) had the Holy Spirit *with* them–*John 14:17*
   b. Since the sending of the Comforter in Acts 2, believers enjoy the presence of the Holy Spirit *in* them–*John 14:17*. See: *John 7:38, 39*
   c. We now receive the Holy Spirit at the moment of salvation–*Romans 8:9, 11; I Corinthians 6:19; II Timothy 1:14; James 4:5; 1 John 9:27; 3:24; 4:4, 13*
   d. According to John 14, believers have:
   - The *Spirit* of God dwelling within them–*verse 17*
   - *Christ* dwelling within them–*verse 20c* See: *Ephesians 3:17; Colossians 1:27*
   - The *Father* and the Son dwelling within them–*verse 23b ("we")*
3. *He gave us His peace–John 14:27; John 16:33*
   a. Peace *with* God comes through justification by faith (salvation)– *Romans 4:25–5:1; Colossians 1:20*
   b. The Peace *of* God comes through the promise that God will hear and answer prayer–*Philippians 4:6, 7*
The world knows nothing of God's Word, God's Spirit, and God's peace. By these, He manifests Himself to us.

III. The Intensity Of Judas:

We assume Judas Lebbaeus Thaddaeus, the brother of James was the human writer of the epistle of Jude. (*Jude 1 identifies its writer as "Jude, the brother of James."*) This being the case, we can gain some additional (and interesting) insight concerning this epistle:

   A. *The Epistle of Jude*–its occasion

The Book of Jude was written later than most other New Testament epistles, after error and apostasy began making serious inroads into the churches–*verse 3*.

B. *The Epistle of Jude*–its content

1. Could Jude have penned these words with the deeds of his infamous namesake (Judas Iscariot) in mind?

    a. Certain men crept in unawares (*verse 4*)–*Matthew 26:22*

    b. Ran greedily after reward (*verse 11*)–*Matthew 26:15*

    c. Spots in your feasts of charity (*verse 12*)–*John 13:26*

    d. Murmurers and complainers (*verse 16*)–*John 12:4, 5*

2. Could Jude have penned this epistle with the blessed promise of Christ to manifest Himself in mind?

    a. God's Word–*verse 17*

    b. God's Presence–*verse 19*

    c. God's Peace–*verse 21*

Consider the similarity between *John 14:23* (*"If a man love me, he will keep my words; and my Father will love him"*) and *Jude 21* (*"Keep yourselves in the love of God…"*.)

3. Could Jude have penned this epistle realizing that he was utterly dependent on the Lord, lest he also betray Him? *Jude 24, 25–"Now unto him that is able to keep you from falling, and to present you faultless before the presence of his glory with exceeding job, To the only wise God our Saviour, be glory and majesty, dominion and power, both now and for ever. Amen."*

The Application:

Judas Lebbaeus Thaddaeus stands in contrast to his infamous namesake Judas Iscariot. The two snippets of information we have about him show this to be the case–when Jesus was present, Judas was most concerned about having and experiencing Christ's presence *after* the Lord returned to glory (hence his question in *John 14:22*); years later he is still faithfully exhorting the saints to experience the same presence of God in the face of growing apostasy. Judas exhibits the qualities of earnestness, steadfastness, and courage. Legend has Judas preaching at Edessa and other areas of Armenia before meeting his death in a hail of arrows near Ararat.

THE LESSON:

> A. *Ask the Question*: "How do we know that Jesus is with us?"
> 1. Teach how Judas Lebbaeus Thaddaeus asked the same question after Jesus spoke of leaving the disciples.
> 2. Relate the story of the first supper, and the events surrounding this apostle's suggestion.
>
> B. *Answer the Question*:
> 1. Explain the teaching of Christ concerning His Word, His Spirit, and His Peace.
> 2. Show how these realities equipped and enabled the apostle to remain faithful to his Master all his life. When teaching children, be sure to use visual aids–pictures, flannel graph, etc.

DISCUSSION:

- How Biblically accurate is it for a Christian to say, "I have Jesus in my heart?"
- Why?
- What does this mean?
- How might Judas Iscariot's betrayal have affected Judas Lebbaeus Thaddaeus?
- How might others have perceived him because of his name?
- What is the best way for a Christian to overcome any poor reflection on his or her reputation?
- Discuss the well-known hymn by C. Austin Miles, *In the Garden*. How do the words of this song reflect the promise of Christ given in response to Judas's question.
- Perhaps the name "Lebbaeus" was given to Judas because of his courage. Why is courage needed to stand uncompromisingly for the Faith?

Judas (Not Iscariot)

Sermon title: The Disciple Who Learned About the Holy Spirit

Text: John 14:21–26

We are studying about a disciple who was known by three different names. He was called "Judas Lebbaeus Thaddaeus," (that's a mouthful) but for the sake of simplicity and sanity we'll just refer to him as the Bible does here in John 14, as Judas (not Iscariot). And as we study an event in Judas's life, you're going to learn about a man who saw the invisible.

John 14:21–26

He that hath my commandments, and keepeth them, he it is that loveth me: and he that loveth me shall be loved of my Father, and I will love him, and will manifest myself to him. Judas saith unto him, no Iscariot, Lord, how is it that thou wilt manifest thyself unto us, and not unto the world? Jesus answered and said unto him, If a man love me, he will keep my words; and my Father will love him, and we will come unto him, and make our abode with him. He that loveth me not keepeth not my sayings; and the word which ye hear is not mine, but the Father's which sent me. These things have I spoken unto you, being yet present with you. But the Comforter, which is the Holy Ghost, whom the Father will send in my name, he shall teach you all things, and bring all things to your remembrance, whatsoever I have said unto you.

Now, Judas Lebbeaus Thaddaeus was an obscure disciple. We know very little about him. As a matter of fact, all that we really now about him is that he asked a question. He asked, "Lord how is it that you are going to make yourself known to your own children? How is it that you are going to make yourself known to those who are saved, those who are born again, but not to the people of the world? What is it that you are going to do for us, and in us and with us that is real and distinct and different? How are we going to know that it's you? How are we going to know that our faith is real? Lord, how are you going to manifest yourself to us?"

And by the way, this is something that we desperately and definitely need to know–that it's real. We have a lot of people today who are just going through the motions. They don't know that their salvation is real.

They don't have the manifestation of the Holy Spirit within them. And I feel sorry for them. I'm like Vance Havner who said, "If you could have it and not know it, you could lose it and not miss it." I believe that you ought to know that you're saved and I believe that God ought to manifest Himself to you. It ought to be real in your heart.

You know, there are so many people that go to church every Sunday and just go through the motions. They endure religion, but they don't enjoy salvation. They don't have the manifestation in their heart. There's no life. There's no joy. There's no reality. There is no manifestation of the presence of God. I want to ask you a question: is God real to you? Is God manifesting Himself to you?

How do you know that you're saved? Is it because you walked down the aisle at some church and gave your hand to some preacher? Or do you have a witness deep down inside of you that lets you know that you are a child of God? The Bible says that there is to be a manifestation. Judas asked, "Lord, how are you going to manifest yourself to us and not to the world?" And, of course, the answer that Jesus gave to him was the Holy Spirit.

Jesus had answered Judas's question before he even asked it. How is the Lord going to manifest Himself to the Christian? By the Holy Spirit of God that lives in his heart. Judas was ignorant of this truth. And there are a lot of people today who are just like Judas, they don't know. They want reality of that relationship, but they're looking for it in all the wrong places.

Some people look to *intellectualism and education*. Now, I'm not against education. I'm for it. You ought to learn and you ought to study. I'm for education, but education can only do so much. I'll tell you this; I'd rather be in heaven saying my ABCs than in hell spouting philosophy.

Other people look to *emotionalism*. They say that the way to know that it's real is to get yourself all worked up emotionally. So they go to worship where there's high powered music and charismatic preaching and all kinds of manipulation techniques. They get themselves all worked up and then they say, "Praise God! I've got it!" But then the next day, all they have is the memory of an experience. And they say, "Man, I sure wish that I could feel today the way that I did yesterday."

Now, I'm not against emotion. I believe in getting excited in church. Listen, I believe that you ought to enjoy your religion. Emotion is alright, but you're not going to know God because of an emotional experience. That's not the kind of manifestation that I'm talking about. You don't discover it in your head through education. You don't discover it through some sort of emotional experience.

I'll tell you something else; you won't find it through *involvement*. You've met these folks; they say things like, "A busy Christian is a happy Christian." Do this. Do that. Go here. Go there. Work on this group. Help out this cause. They're wearing themselves out trying to be good Christians. But that's not where you find this kind of manifestation that Jesus is talking about here.

I'll tell you another place you won't find it and that's in *legalism*. That's nothing but being a Pharisee. You now what the Pharisee says. He says, "The way to be a good Christian is by giving up all of the things of the world. Don't do this and don't do that." Now listen, the things of the world ought to be given up, but that's not the answer. You see, if all you do is give up worldly things without having the witness of the Holy Spirit in your heart, you become a hard, bitter Pharisee. Being a victorious Christian isn't found in just giving up things.

You say, "Alright pastor, what is the answer? How am I going to know that God is real in my life? Well, the answer is by the presence of the Holy Spirit. God is going to come into your heart, into your life by His Holy Spirit, and His Holy Spirit is going to manifest the life of God in you. You will know that it's real and you're going to rejoice in it because you have inside information.

Let's see what Judas learned about the Holy Spirit.

Judas Learned About the Person of the Holy Spirit

He has personality. Who is the Holy Spirit? Well, He is the third person of the Trinity. Now, when I say that He's third, I don't mean that He takes third place. He is co-equal and co-eternal with God the Father and God the Son. In other words, He's not an "it." He's a person.

He's the third person in the Trinity. You say, "Pastor, I can't understand the Trinity." Welcome to the club. I don't understand how cable television works. Maybe there are some who understand it, but I don't. That doesn't mean that I can't enjoy it. Listen, don't you be guilty of putting God in your suitcase sized mind and then cutting off everything that doesn't fit.

Listen, God is God and there is no way that you can explain Him.

There's no way that you can fully comprehend Him. He says, *"I am God, to who shall you liken and compare me?"*

I like what an old country preacher said, "If you try to define the Trinity you'll lose your mind. If you deny the Trinity you'll lose your soul."

Now, there are some false teachers, some cults who are running around today and knocking on doors claiming to be teachers of the Word of God, and yet they deny the Biblical teaching of the reality of the Holy Spirit. They say that He's not a person. They say that the Holy Spirit is an influence that comes from God. Listen, the Holy Spirit is more than an influence. He's more than a force. He is a person.

Do you know what the Bible says? The Bible says that you can blaspheme the Holy Ghost. You can't blaspheme an influence. You can't blaspheme a force. You can only blaspheme a divine person. He can be blasphemed. That's the unpardonable sin.

I'll tell you something else. The Bible says in Ephesians 4:30 that *you can grieve the Holy Spirit.* Now, you can't grieve a thing. You can't grieve an influence. You can't grieve a force. Only a person can be grieved.

He has intelligence. Romans 8:27 says, *"Now He who searches the hearts knows what the mind of the Spirit is…"* Now, an influence doesn't have a mind, but a person does.

He has emotions. He can be grieved. *Romans 5:5* says that *"the love of God has been poured out in our hearts by the Holy Spirit who was given to us."*

He has a will. The Holy Spirit has a will just like any person has a will. Read in *Acts 13:2*. The Bible says that *"As they ministered to the Lord and fasted, the Holy Spirit said, "Now separate to Me Barnabas and Saul for the work to which I have called them."* It was the Holy Spirit that commissioned the church's mission movement.

So, the first thing that Judas learned on that day was that the Holy Spirit is a person.

Judas Learned About the Purpose of the Holy Spirit

What is the purpose of the Holy Spirit? The purpose of the Holy Spirit is to take Jesus's place here on this earth. Look at what Jesus said:

John 14:16–18
And I will pray the Father, and he shall give you another Comforter, that

he may abide with you for ever; Even the Spirit of truth; whom the world cannot receive, because it seeth him not, neither knoweth him but ye know him; for he dwelleth with you, and shall be in you. I will not leave you comfortless: I will come to you.

The Holy Spirit is Christ in the Christian

That's who the Holy Spirit is, but now, what does the Holy Spirit do? What is the work of the Holy Spirit within you?

He is the substance of your life. The new life that you have when you receive Christ is really the life of the Spirit. The Bible says in *2 Peter 1:4* that we are *"partakers of the divine nature."* Now, when do we become partakers of the divine nature? When the Holy Spirit comes into us. The Bible says in *Romans 8:9*, *"Now if anyone does not have the Spirit of Christ, he is not His."* And then the Bible says in *Romans 8:16* that, *"The Spirit Himself bears witness with our spirit that we are children of God."* You see, the Holy Spirit is the substance of our lives.

He is the seal of your security. The Bible says in *Ephesians 1:13* that after you believe you are "sealed" with the Holy Spirit. And the Bible says in *Ephesians 4:30* about that seal that we are *"sealed until the day of redemption."* That means when God saved me He put His seal upon me.

What that means to the average Christian is this. Once I am saved, I am always saved. Some folks say, "Well, I can't believe that. That's why I could never be a Baptist. I could never believe that "once saved always saved stuff." Listen, I stay saved because God is holding on to me.

That's why Jesus said:

John 10:27–29

"My sheep hear my voice, and I know them, and they follow me: And I give unto them eternal life; and they shall never perish, neither shall any man pluck them out of my hand. My Father, which gave them me, is greater than all and no man is able to pluck them out of my Father's hand."

He is the secret of your victory. How are you going to live the victorious Christian life? How are you going to live victoriously over sin? Read *Romans 8:2*, *"For the law of the Sprit of life in Christ Jesus has made me free from the law of sin and death."*

He is the strength of your service. The Bible says in *Acts 1:8*, *"But you shall receive power when the Holy Spirit has come upon you."* I'm telling you that I would rather die than to try and preach without the power and anointing of the Holy Ghost of God. I am glad that God gives us supernatural power to live for Him, preach for Him, witness for Him and serve Him.

He is the spring of your joy. How many really happy people do you know today? What does the Bible say? *But the fruit of the Spirit is love, joy…"* He's the spring of the Christians' joy.

He is the source of your knowledge

John 15:26

But when the Comforter is come, whom I will send unto you from the Father, even the Spirit of truth, which proceedeth from the Father, he shall testify of me.

John 14:26

But the Comforter, which is the Holy Ghost, whom the Father will send in my name, he shall teach you all things, and bring all things to your remembrance, whatsoever I have said unto you.

When you get saved, you get your own, personal tutor that comes to live inside of you. He teaches you all things.

How can you read and understand and get out of the Bible what God wants you to get out of it?

I Corinthians 2:14

But the natural man receiveth not the things of the Spirit of God; for they are foolishness unto him: neither can he know them, because they are spiritually discerned.

The Holy Spirit is the one who makes real to you what Christ purchased for you on the Cross. What a shame if you didn't know it! What a shame if you didn't understand it! And how are you going to know, how is it going to be made manifest in your life? The Holy Spirit is going to teach you.

Judas Learned About the Power of the Holy Spirit

How are you going to have this wonderful, precious Holy Spirit working freely in your heart and in your life? Why is it that some Christians seem to know the Lord more than others?

John 14:23

Jesus answered and said unto him, "If a man love me, he will keep my words; and my Father will love him, and we will come unto him, and make our abode with him.

The way to be filled with the Holy Spirit is to love Jesus enough to obey him. The Bible says that God gives the Holy Spirit to those who obey him. Now, the Holy Spirit is resident in every believer, but He's not president in every Believer's Life. It's one thing for Him to just abide, it's another thing for Him to preside.

The promises of God are tied to the commands of God. When we start living obediently to the Lord, the Holy Spirit begins to work power in our life.

SIMON ZELOTES

The Zealous Apostle

Lesson Text:

Luke: 12–16

Study Texts:

Matthew 10:4; Mark 3:18; Luke 6:15; Acts 1:13

Memory Verse:

Galatians 4:18–"But it is good to be zealously affected always in a good thing, and not only when I am present with you.

The Study:

Apart from being mentioned in the four apostolic lists, nothing is said about this apostle. He is known more for *what* he was then *who* he was!

I. The Nickname Of Simon:

The name Simon (from the Hebrew "Simeon") was a fairly common name. There are *eight* other Simons mentioned in the New Testament:

    1. Simon Peter (*Matthew 4:18; Acts 15:14*)–an apostle

    2. The step-brother of the Lord (*Matthew 13:55*)

    3. Simon the Leper (*Matthew 26:6*)–lived in Bethany

    4. Simon the Cyrene (*Matthew 27:32*)–bore the cross

    5. Simon the Pharisee (*Luke 7:39, 40*)

    6. Judas Iscariot's father (*John 6:17*)

    7. Simon Magus (*Acts 8:9, 13, 18–24*)–the sorcerer.

    8. Simon the Tanner (*Acts 9:43*)

In addition to these, there are two Simeons:

    1. Simeon of Jerusalem (*Luke 2:25*)

    2. Simeon the black man (*Acts 13:1*)–a pastor at Antioch

The Apostle Simon was delineated by two nicknames:

    A. *The Canaanite–Matthew 10:4; Mark 3:18*

1. He was not a Canaanite by race–the apostles were all Israelites
2. He may have been called a Canaanite because of:
    a. Where he lived
    b. His appearance
        We just do not know
3. Some have thought the Greek word translated Canaanite (*kananites* [not the regular '*chananaios*'–'of Canaan']) was derived from the Hebrew verb *kana* meaning "jealous.")

B. *Zelotes–Luke 6:15; Acts 1:13*
1. The Greek word "*zelos*" ranges in meaning from "jealousy" and "emulation" to "fervor" and "ambition."
2. Simon was called "Zelotes" because of his zeal–his passionate enthusiasm.
3. Because of this, it is thought by some that Simon was previously associated with a group of Jewish patriots known as Zealots–freedom fighters dedicated to resisting the Roman occupation. (This movement arose out of previously failed attempts by Jews to overthrow Rome (*Acts 5:36, 37*), and actually brought on the final destruction of Jerusalem and the Jewish Diaspora in 70 a.d.)
4. The question is: Was Simon called "Zelotes" before he was saved, baptized, and called to be an apostle? Or, was he called Zelotes by the other apostles? Again, we just do not know.
5. Legend has Simon later preaching in Persia, and meeting his end by crucifixion.

II. The Zeal Of Simon:

Zeal is like a fire–it needs both feeding and watching! Zeal can be biblically directed or misdirected.

A. *Misdirected Zeal*:
Many people are zealous but for the wrong cause. Perhaps Simon was indeed a radical insurrectionist–seeking to bring in the kingdom of God through the violent overthrow of Rome. If this was so, his zeal was certainly

misdirected. Cults are zealous. Islam is zealous. New-age environmentalists are zealous. Many involved in wicked causes are zealous. This is misdirected zeal.

1. *Zeal alone cannot bring salvation*: Many have the idea that it doesn't matter what you believe so long as you are sincere (zealous) about it. However:
    a. Zeal would not save the Jews–*Romans 10:1–4*
    b. Zeal could not save Saul of Tarsus–*Acts 22:3; Galatians 1:14; Philippians 3:6 7*
    c. Zeal cannot save religious professors–*Matthew 7:15–23*

2. *Christians can be zealously caught up in wrong things.*
    a. Zealous over false doctrine–*Galatians 3:1; 4:8–10, 17*
    b. Zealous in flaunting their perceived spirituality–*I Corinthians 14:12; I Corinthians 13:1–3*

3. *Christians can be overly-zealous in right things*
    a. Peter zealously sought to protect Christ, for which he was rebuked–*John 18:10*
    b. We can be so zealous in our liberty that we cause a weaker brother to stumble–*I Corinthians 8:9–13*

B. *Biblically Directed Zeal*:

There are some things we need to be zealous about:

1. Zealous for the Word of God–*Psalms119:139, 140; Acts 17:11; Job 23:12*
2. Zealous in Prayer–*James 5:16; Colossians 4:12; I Thessalonians 3:10; II Timothy 1:3*
3. Zealous over the House of God–*Psalm 69:9; I Timothy 3:15; Hebrews 10:25*
4. Zealous in Giving–*II Corinthians 9: 2, 13*
5. Zealous of Good Works–*Titus 2:11–14; Romans 12:11; Ecclesiastes 9:10; Colossians 3:23; Philippians 2:30*
6. Zealous toward the saints–*Colossians 4:13; I Corinthians 6:15; I Peter 4:8 Colossians 4:13; I Corinthians 6:15; I Peter 4:8*
7. Zealous for Church Purity–*Revelation 3:19*. Note the attitude of the church at Corinth when taking disciplinary

action, *II Corinthians 7:11*. This action was designated to preserve the purity of the bride (*I Corinthians 5:5, 6*).

The Application:

Whether Simon was a political zealot who became a follower (and later an apostle) of the Lord Jesus Christ, *or* an apostle who came to be noted for his zeal–the fact remains: zeal rightly directed is a precious commodity so desperately needed in today's climate of spiritual apathy, indifference, and slothfulness.

The Lesson:

A. *The Story of Simon*
  1. Show where Simon is listed with the twelve apostles
  2. Point out that he is called "Zealotes," and what that means

B. *Zeal*

Since the Word of God provides no historical information about Simon, this will be a lesson on zeal. Zeal is a somewhat abstract word, so it will need to be carefully explained to younger children. This is best done by using (relevant) examples of zeal. Perhaps the best example is of a sports fan ("fan" comes from the shortened "fanatic!")

Use Galatians 4:17, 18 to teach the different kinds of zeal:
  1. Zealously affected, but not well–the *wrong* kind of zeal.
  2. It is good to be zealously affected in a good thing–the *right* kind of zeal.
  3. Not only when I am present with you–the *best* kind of zeal.

Discussion:

- There are two dangerous extremes: Ignorance on Fire, and Knowledge on Ice. Why should these be avoided by Christians?
- How does a lack of real zeal affect:
  » Evangelism?
  » Christian Love?
  » Holiness?

- By what means and in what ways can zeal be restored in a church of the Lord Jesus Christ?
- By what means and in what ways can zeal be *maintained in a church of the Lord Jesus Christ?*
- What are the biggest "zeal extinguishers" in your life?

Simon the Zealot

Sermon Title: A Man on Fire

Text: Luke 6:15

Simon was one of the most interesting of the 12 disciples. All we know about him is his name, but that one little piece of information paints for us a picture of a man who was on fire for Jesus. This was a man who was converted for a purpose and consumed with a passion for his Lord. His name was Simon the Zealot.

We don't know where Simon came from. We don't know anything that he did nor have any words recorded that he said. We don't even know for sure where he ended up–where or how he died. The only thing that we know about him for sure is his name and this title.

In *Luke 6:15* he's referred to as *"Simon called the Zealot."* In *Acts 1:13* he's called *"Simon the Zealot."* And in *Matthew 10:4* and *Mark 3:18* he's given the title, *"Simon the Canaanite."* And what these titles refer to is a personality that was passionate, a disciple that was fiery, and an emotion that was literally boiling over, because that's what the word "zealot" means. It means "to boil." It means "to seethe," "to fume," even "to rage."

So, with that, let me share with you three simple truths that we can learn from this man on fire by the name of Simon the Zealot.

He Loved His God and Country

You see, that little phrase there, "the Zealot" is more than a description; it's a designation and a definition. It tells us that here was a man who was completely consumed with a nationalistic zeal for his country. That's why he was called a "zealot."

Today we have Republicans, Democrats and Independents, but back in those days they had 5 main political/religious parties that were in power in Judea.

There were the Pharisees. These were the religious fundamentalists of their time. They were extremely conservative when it came to the rules and regulations of the law.

There were the Sadducees. They were the liberal religious group of that day who denied the supernatural. They were also rich, powerful and in charge of the Temple.

There were the Essenes. They were the independents who lived out in the desert and devoted themselves to the study of the Law.

There were the Herodians, those who were loyal to Herod.

And then there were the Zealots. Who were the Zealots? Well, in essence, they were the Pharisees of the Pharisees. They were more politically minded than any of these other groups and they lived out there in the far right wing of the political landscape of that day.

These Zealots had a fiery, fervent, and fanatical love for God and country. When they were at their best they would have the character and the qualities of freedom fighters from any generation, be it the colonial army standing up against British occupation, or the French underground resistance in WW2.

Now, the Bible doesn't give us much information abut these fanatics called Zealots, other than this title given to Simon and the mention of the death of one of their leaders in Acts chapter 5. So, basically what we know about them comes mostly from secular history through a Jewish historian by the name of Josephus. He says that during the time of Jesus, there was a Jewish Nationalist Party that was called the "Zealots."

The Zealots hated the Romans (and anybody who compromised or collaborated, went along to get along with the Romans) and their goal was to overthrow Roman occupation and bring about the Messianic kingdom that they read about in the prophecies of the Old Testament. You see, they believed that not only had Rome destroyed the independence of Israel, they believed that Rome's pagan influence was permeating their culture and making it difficult for them to keep the law and observe many of the ceremonies that were set forth in the Law of Moses.

They worked, fought, planned and prayed for a Messiah who would restore the Kingdom of Israel and return the glory of the Old Theocracy that had once been the distinguishing mark of their nation.

So, here was a man who by his very title is described as a man who had a red hot, raging, boiling, burning love for God and country.

He Was Loyal To His Group's Cause

Evidently he wasn't just your average, everyday, run of the mill

Zealot. Here was a man who carried and conveyed his group's cause in his very name.

Now, just in case you haven't realized it yet, when the writers of Scripture refer to this man as a "Zealot," they weren't paying him a compliment. It was like calling Matthew a tax collector or Judas the traitor. As a matter of fact, this was a slur, a slam, and a statement of derision. Josephus, that Jewish historian that I mentioned a moment ago, even referred to them as "irreconcilables." And the reason for that was because of the history and the activity of this particular party.

Let me share with you more about this group that this man by the name of Simon belonged to. You see, not only did they revolt and rebel against Roman rule and Roman domination in Judea, they actually resorted to murder and terrorism and plunder in order to accomplish their goals.

The Romans and others called them "dagger men" or "assassins" because of the deadly, curved daggers that they carried in the folds of their robes. They would sneak up behind Roman soldiers and politicians, and for that matter, any Jew they felt was collaborating with their oppressors. They would stab them in the back, between the ribs, expertly piercing the heart. They carried out guerilla-style attacks across Judea and then would retreat back to their headquarters in Galilee. They were hated and hunted, fought and feared. These were the men that caused young Roman children to fear the dark. They had the reputation of slipping in during the middle of the night and killing the families of those they saw as being their enemies.

So hot was their hatred and so deadly was their determination to throw off Roman rule, that history tells us that they were willing to suffer any kind of death (crucifixion, decapitation, being burned at the stake, thrown into the coliseum to face wild animals) or endure any amount of pain without uttering a word. They would even sacrifice any member of their family; commit any kind of terrible act in order to secure their religious and political freedom.

I want you to see what kind of a character Simon was before he met Jesus. He was a fanatic. He was a terrorist. He was a militant. Most likely he was a murderer. He had probably committed all kinds of crimes against Rome and even his fellow Jews. Not only did He love his God and country. Not only was he loyal to his group's cause, but after meeting Jesus…

He Lived For the Glory of Christ

We're not told how or when He met Christ. We're not told about his conversion like we are some of the other disciples. We don't know the circumstances that caused him to forsake all and follow Christ. We know that he did. He met Jesus and Jesus totally transformed his life. He left a group known for death and became part of a group that was concerned with life. He became one of the 12 disciples.

How do I know that he left all? How do I know that he forsook his former life to pursue a better life? How do I know that he wasn't just hooking up with this group because he thought that Jesus was going to be the one that overthrew Roman domination and bring about the restoration of the Kingdom like the Zealots were working for? I'll tell you how. Jesus taught them to pay their taxes to Rome. He said, *"Render to Caesar the things that are Caesars."* A true Zealot would never have gone for that. Remember when Jesus was talking about how far to go when somebody is abusing you? What did He say? *"If someone forces you to go one mile, go with him two miles."* Do you know what He was talking about? A Roman soldier could pick you out of the crowd and force you to carry his load, and Jesus said if they do that, literally *"go the extra mile."* A Zealot would never have bought that.

However, the thing that really lets me know that Simon was a changed man is the fact that he ate and slept and walked and worked with a Roman tax collector by the name of Matthew. That's the thing that sticks out in my mind and proves to me that Jesus had totally transformed his life. Instead of murdering Matthew, he ministered with him.

So, here's the point of the whole sermon. This is what I want you to learn from the life of Simon the Zealot. When you come to Jesus and Jesus saves you, He doesn't change your personality, but He does channel your passion. I mean, after Simon followed Jesus, they still called him a zealot. I think that wasn't just talking about his politics; it was a statement about his personality. Here was a man who was just as hot hearted, fiery, and passionate about things as he ever was. It's just that instead of living for this world, He was looking for a world to come. Instead of trying to liberate Jerusalem and restore its glory, he gave the rest of his life trying to bring glory to Jesus.

Jesus took his zeal and gave it direction and passion and gave it purpose—and Jesus can do the same work in your life today.

On August 7, 1994, a 5,200-horsepower locomotive pulled twenty-four cars from Chicago to Fort Wayne, Indiana and back. On board the train were 846 passengers. The passengers weren't in a hurry to reach their destination because their interest wasn't in travel, per se, but in the train. Most were members of the National Historic Railway Society.

Powering this train was a Class J, No. 611 steam locomotive. Now, steam locomotives may sound very old fashioned, but they are also very powerful. As a matter of fact, some of the old steam locomotives were more powerful than three modern diesel locomotives.

The heart of their power, of course, is steam. Steam is "water turned to gas," wrote Kate Eaton.

"You may think you see it above your whistling tea kettle or on your bathroom mirror, but that's not it. Steam is the clear vapor between the hot water and the visible mist. As it forms at 212 degrees Fahrenheit, it expands to take up much more space than its liquid state. This explosive expansion, harnessed in a giant locomotive, is what powered 250 ton engines pulling 20 or more railcars through the Blue Ridge Mountains, across the Great Plains and over the deserts of the west. "It's a powerful force," said Robert Pinsky, of the Railway Society.

Just as steam gives power to a locomotive, so zeal gives power to a believer. The more we boil with zeal for Christ, the more power we have for service.

ANDREW

The Apostle Who Brought Others to Christ

LESSON TEXT:

John 1:35–42

STUDY TEXTS:

Matthew 4:18; Matthew 10:2; Mark 1:16; Mark 3:18; Luke 6:14; John 1:35–42; John 12:20–22, Acts 1:13

MEMORY VERSE:

John 1:41, 42a–"He first findeth his own brother Simon, and saith unto him, We have found the Messiah, which is, being interpreted, the Christ. And he brought him to Jesus."

THE STUDY:

I. Andrew's Background:
    A. *His Name*
        The name "Andrew" comes from the Greek (*andreas*) and means "manly."
    B. *His Family*
        1. He was the brother of Simon Peter–e.g. *Matthew 10:2*
        2. His father's name was Jona–*John 1:42*
        3. Andrew lived in Bethsaida–*John 1:44*
    C. *His Occupation*
        Andrew was a fisherman–*Matthew 4:18*
    D. *His Life As a Believer*
        1. *His Conversion*–Andrew was a disciple of John the Baptist, *John 1:35, 40.* This means he was saved and baptized under the ministry of John.
        2. *His Discipleship*–Andrew became a follower of Christ immediately after John pointed out the Messiah to him, *John 1:36, 37* Andrew is called "*protokletos*"–i.e., "first called."

3. *His Call to "Full-time" Service*–Andrew later left his fishing business to follow Christ continually, *Matthew 4:18; mark 1:16–18.*
4. *His Call to Be an Apostle*–*Luke 6:13, 14*
5. *His Subsequent Ministry*
   a. The apostles remained together in Jerusalem up to the time of Saul's conversion (*Acts 8:1, 14; 9:27.*) Apostles were still present in Jerusalem after that (*Acts 11:1; 15:2, 4, 6, 22, 23, 33*), although by then some were traveling (*Acts 9:32; 11:2*).
   b. Tradition has Andrew preaching in Asia Minor and north of the Black Sea. Because of this, he is today known as the "patron saint" of Russia.
   c. Another tradition has Andrew meeting his death in Patras in Greece, being scourged before being nailed to a diagonal cross. Because of this, Andrew is also the "patron saint" of Greece.
   d. An 8th century a.d. tradition has a Catholic monk taking parts of Andrew's relics (bones) to Scotland (St. Andrews). Because of this, Andrew is also the "patron saint" of Scotland.

E. *His Standing*

Andrew stands in the shadow of his well-known brother, Simon Peter.
1. He is often referred to as Peter's brother–*Matthew 4:18; 10:2; Mark 1:16; Luke 6:14; John 1:40; 6:8.* Yet it was Andrew who brought Peter to Christ!
2. He was not part of the "inner circle"–though he may have been on the fringe, *Mark 13:3.* Yet Andrew was the first to be called by Christ.
3. Andrew is listed in Matthew, Mark, and Luke, but the only accounts of Andrew actually *doing* something are recorded in John's Gospel. (Perhaps John could relate to being the "second string" in a fraternal relationship!) It requires a true Christian spirit (*John 3:30*) to accept a ministry role that (by human reckoning) is "second string," "behind the scenes." See: *I Corinthians 3:5–7;*

4:1–7; Romans 12:3. Caleb, one of two faithful and courageous Israelite spies, never received any position or glory (like the other spy, Joshua)–yet he remained wholehearted and steadfast for another 40+ years (*Joshua 14:6–14*). He never became bitter or resentful.

II. Andrew's Notable Characteristic:

Whenever we read of Andrew doing something, it is always bringing others to Jesus Christ.

A. *Andrew Brought Peter to Christ–John 1:35–42*

This passage is more often than not presented as an example of soul winning. In actual fact however, Peter (like Andrew) was already saved. Both brothers were already followers of John the Baptist. There are some great principles in this passage which apply just as well to winning the lost to Christ:

1. *The Preparation–"They came and saw… and abode with Him" (vs 39)*. Time spent with the Lord is essential for the soul winner. The tenth hour would be around 4 p.m., two hours before sundown.

2. *The Priority–"He first findeth his own brother"* (*vs 41*). Winning others to Christ is the first priority of every believer. This is by virtue of the Great Commission given by Christ to His churches–*Matthew 28:18–20; Mark 16:15*.

3. *The Persistence–"He first FINDETH his own brother" (vs 41)*.

They will not come–they must be brought
They will not seek–they must be sought
They will not learn–they must be taught

Winning others to Christ involves effort. We must *go*. See: *Luke 15:4*.

4. *The Plan–"He first findeth his own brother" (vs 41.)*. Just as the master plan for *world* evangelism began in Jerusalem (home) then radiated out into Judea, Samaria, and the uppermost farthest parts of the earth (*Acts 1:8*), so the master plan for *personal* evangelism ought to begin at home, then radiate out from there.

5. *The Proclamation–"We have found the Messiah… the Christ"* (*vs 41*). Here we see the value of personal testimony. A witness is one who has seen or experienced something personally. *John 9:25b–"One thing I know, that, whereas I was blind, now I see."*
6. *The Purpose–"He brought him to JESUS"* (*vs 42*). Sinners need Christ. They don't need a creed, or even a church–they need the Lord! See: *Acts 14:6: Acts 4:12.*
7. *The Prize–"Thou shalt be called Cephas"* (*vs 42*). God has a unique plan for *every* soul who is born again. He did for Peter! The Great Commission doesn't end with winning someone to Christ. Salvation is the beginning of everlasting life in Christ–believers must be led into discipleship and on to Christian maturity. See: *Hebrews 6:1–3; II Peter 3:18.*

B. *Andrew Brought a lad to Christ–John 6:1–13.*

While Philip was counting up all the loose change the apostles could come up with, Andrew found a young boy who was willing to offer his lunch to Christ. *John 6:9* suggests three things about Andrew:

1. *He was "people-oriented."*
The Lord Jesus Christ had actually asked all the apostles to find out how many loaves were available (*Mark 6:38*), but only Andrew was successful. *Attitude* probably had a lot to do with it–after all, the apostles had wanted to "get rid" of the problem by sending the great multitude away (*Matthew 14:15*). *Sinners are not the problem–they're the prize!* How else did Andrew know about the young boy if he wasn't actively getting among the people?

2. *He was optimistic*
Andrew didn't know the how or why, but he knew Jesus Christ is able to take and use anything that is offered willingly. *No one is of no use to the Lord!*

3. *He was dependent on Christ to do something great.*
Andrew's question, *"But what are they among so many?"* was not one of despair, but rather of expectation. It was a question anticipating something from the Lord, much

like Mary's statement to Jesus in *John 2:3* ("*They have no wine,*" implying, "What are you going to do about it?")

C. *Andrew Brought Greeks to Christ–John 12:20–22*
(*See the notes for this reference under the Apostle Philip*)
1. Andrew had surely been made into a "fisher of men!" These Greeks were (despised) Gentiles, yet Andrew reached out to help bring them to Christ.
2. Now, Andrew is helping another brother become a soul winner too.

The Application:

The story of the apostle Andrew has a two-fold application:

The priority of bringing others to Christ. This must be foremost in all that we do (*II Corinthians 5:11, 14*). It is a wise thing to do (*Proverbs 11:30b*). It is an essential thing to do (*Ezekiel 3:18; I Corinthians 1:18.*) It is a compassionate thing to do (*Jude 22, 23*).

The value of those who labor "behind the scenes." Andrew no doubt lived in the shadow of his more famous and outspoken brother, yet he was a tremendous blessing to others. Read: *Romans 16:1–16* to see the importance of such people. (The same applies within the membership of a church, *I Corinthians 12:14–27*.) The apostle Paul is considered to be the greatest church-planting evangelist ever, yet he always worked with a *team*–others he referred to as his *fellow soldiers, fellow labourers, fellow workers, fellow servants,* and even *fellow prisoners.* Of those who surrounded him we generally know very little, yet they were vital to the Lord's work.

The Lesson:

A. *God's Plan and Purpose*
1. What does the Lord want His churches to do more than anything else? (*Mark 16:15*).
2. What did Jesus want to make of His disciples? (*Matthew 4:19*).
3. Show how the apostle Andrew fulfilled the Lord's desire for his life. When teaching children, always use visual aids–flannel graph, pictures, objects, etc.

B. *Bringing Others to Jesus*
1. We don't have to be a "big shot." An unnamed

boy was willing to let Jesus take what he had to feed the multitude. A little-known apostle became well- known for introducing others to the Lord.

2. How to bring others to Christ–teach some elementary ways your class members can do this (giving to missions, praying for others, inviting to church/Sunday School, giving a tract, personal witness, etc.) Challenge your class to take soul winning seriously. If appropriate, plan some activities to provide an opportunity for them to actually experience personal witnessing. Do they know what Scriptures to use to lead someone to Christ?

DISCUSSION:

- Statistically, about 2% of believers were first reached through Gospel tracts or advertising, 6% through a pastoral visit, 6% through a visitation contact–but 85% through family and/or friends.

- How were you reached for Christ?

- How many people were involved pointing you to the Saviour?

- Who was the greatest influence in your salvation? How were they like Andrew?

- Does being a "behind-the-scenes" kind of Christian remove any obligation of actually seeking to personally win others to Christ? Why?

Andrew

Title: The Master's Man

Text: John 1:35–40

> *Again the next day after John stood, and two of his disciples; And looking upon Jesus as he walked, he saith, Behold the Lamb of God! And the two disciples heard him speak, and they followed Jesus. Then Jesus turned, and saw them following, and saith unto them, What seek ye? They said unto him, Rabbi, (which is to say, being interpreted, master,) where dwellest thou? He saith unto them, Come and see. They came and saw where he dwelt, and abode with him that day; for it was about the tenth hour. One of the two which heard John speak, and followed him, was Andrew, Simon Peter's brother.*

In this message we are studying about Andrew, who was the very first one of these 12 men to follow Jesus. Andrew was Simon Peter's brother and was normally introduced in this way. However, these two men were very different in their personality. They were complete opposites. Peter was bold and brash, while Andrew was calm and considerate.

As far as we know, Andrew never preached to great big crowds. He was even excluded from some of the events that Peter, James and John were allowed to be a part of, and yet in spite of that, there was a consistent, conscientious walk in this man by the name of Andrew. He would be a great example for us to follow because most of us have a better shot at being an Andrew than we do a Peter.

We don't know quite as much about Andrew as we do about Peter. But, we do know that…

He was Simon Peter's brother (*John 1:40*)

He was from Bethsaida (*John 1:44*)

He was a fisherman (*Matthew 4:18*)

He moved to Capernaum and started a fishing business with Peter, James and John (*Matthew 4:13*)

He was a disciple of John the Baptist (*John 1:35*)

He was the first to follow Jesus (*John 1:41*)

He had a very special relationship with Jesus (*Mark 13:3*)

Every time he is mentioned in the gospel of John, he's bringing somebody to Jesus

He was calm and considerate

He was naturally helpful

His name means, "manly."

Now, I just want to stop right there and be real honest. Normally, when we think of a "manly man" we would think of somebody like Peter. We may not think of a man who says "excuse me" or waits for somebody else to go first. Rather, we think of "manly" being like Simon, a guy who'll pull out his sword and take off the ear of the first one who gets near Jesus. However, Jesus changed Simon's name to Peter in order to encourage him and remind him to become something he wasn't as of yet, a man with a rock-solid faith.

Jesus left Andrew's name along because he already was a real man. There are three things that I want you to see from the example of Andrew that can help you to be the real man, or woman, that Jesus desires or you to be.

Real Men Love Jesus

John 1:35–39

Again the next day after John stood, and two of his disciples; And looking upon Jesus as he walked, he saith, Behold the Lamb of God! And the two disciples heard him speak, and they followed Jesus. Then Jesus turned, and saw them following, and saith unto them, What seek ye? They said unto him, Rabbi, (which is to say, being interpreted, master,) where dwellest thou? He saith unto them, Come and see. They came and saw where he dwelt, and abode with him that day; for it was about the tenth hour.

Now, get the picture. Andrew had become a disciple of John the Baptist. Then, one day he heard John the Baptist preach, and say, "*Behold! The Lamb of God who takes away the sin of the world!*" Andrew looked up and saw Jesus and he never looked back. At that moment, Andrew realized who Jesus was and followed Him the rest of his life. He gave up his fishing business to follow Him. He gave up everything else that he had in this world to follow Jesus. He endured hardship and hatred, ridicule and rejection, lack of comfort and the loss of companion, all because of his great love for his Lord.

The greatest thing any man could ever do in your life is love Jesus. You see, somehow society has sown this idea in our minds that church and Christianity is something that's good for women and children, but not for men. Sundays have become the time when women and children go to church and the men go to the couch; women and children go to Sunday School and the men go to the deer stand, the garage or the yard. That's what society says, and it's dead wrong.

The most manly, masculine, and mature thing you could ever do is love Jesus with all of your heart, to follow Him and learn from Him. As a matter of fact, I'm going to show you at the end of this message how much of a man Andrew was and how much he loved his Lord. But for now, you get this truth down and get it down real good–real men love Jesus!

Real Men Lead Others to Jesus

You see, Andrew's love for the Lord compelled him to lead others to love Jesus as well. That's what loving Jesus will cause any person to do. You will have a desire to see others come to love Jesus.

Now, since we're going to be talking here about witnessing and evangelism here, let me tell you one of the tremendous truths that I learned from Andrew, and really it's an indictment from the lips of a quiet man. The reason more Christians aren't bringing people to Jesus like they ought to is because they don't love Jesus like they ought to. You see, bringing people to Jesus is not a matter of knowing how as much as it is a matter of knowing Him.

Andrew loved Jesus and he loved those around him. It was just a natural thing for him to take the hand of his family member or friend and bring them to Jesus. He started where he was by telling his family about Jesus.

John 1:41, 42

He first findeth his own brother Simon, and saith unto him, We have found the Messiah, which is, being interpreted, the Christ. And he brought him to Jesus. And when Jesus beheld him, he said, Thou art Simon the son of Jona: thou shalt be called Cephas, which is by interpretation, A stone.

We usually think about Peter as being the spiritual father of Pentecost, and that's true. But if Peter was the spiritual father of Pentecost, then Andrew was its spiritual grandfather, because he's the one that the Bible says brought Peter to Jesus.

Now, I want you to think about the fact that Andrew brought Peter to Jesus. Do you realize how big, how selfless, how gracious, how loving that one act was? All of his life he had lived in Simon's shadow. All of his life he had to play second fiddle to his louder, bolder brother. But Andrew doesn't get bitter; he develops a heart for spiritual things.

He even takes a sabbatical of sorts from the fishing business to become a disciple of John the Baptist. He's out there learning about spiritual things while Peter's making a living catching fish. And then one day, Andrew runs into Jesus and becomes His first disciple. Do you realize how important that must have been to Andrew? No longer was he in second place. No longer was he taking the back seat to Simon. No longer was he playing second fiddle. He was the first disciple of Jesus, but that wasn't enough. Andrew went and got his brother and brought him to Jesus. And from that day on he faded into the background of the 12, but he's still one of the greatest soul-winners this world has ever known.

Andrew later played an important part in one of the greatest miracles that Jesus ever performed. He really wasn't trying to be a part of a miracle; he was just trying to bring somebody to Jesus.

John 6:8–9

One of his disciples, Andrew, Simon Peter's brother, saith unto him, There is a lad here, which hath five barley loaves, and two small fishes; but what are they among so many?

Andrew had time for this little boy. As a pastor, I love to see people using their gift for God's glory. I love to hear people sing and to hear gifted teachers teach the Word. But, it really touches my heart when somebody takes an interest in a little boy or a little girl or some hardened man or some calloused woman and says, "I may not get to be on stage, I may not have my name in lights, but I'm at least going to try and bring them to Jesus."

But Andrew didn't stop there. He began with his family. He moved out from his family and friends to his neighbors and those he worked with.

John 12:20–22

And there were certain Greeks among them that came up to worship at the feast: The same came therefore to Philip, which was of Bethsaida of Galilee, and desired him, saying, Sir, we would see Jesus. Philip cometh and telleth Andrew; and again Andrew and Philip tell Jesus.

Wow! They had tried the dead formalism of religion, but it didn't satisfy their soul. They came to Philip and Philip came to Andrew and Andrew went to Jesus.

Do you know what Andrew was doing, even though he hadn't heard it yet? He was simply following the pattern of Jesus's Great Commission. *"But you shall receive power when the Holy Spirit has come upon you; and you shall be witnesses to Me in Jerusalem, and in all Judea and Samaria, and to the end of the earth."* He didn't start way out there with person x that he didn't know. He didn't hop on a boat and go all the way around the world to tell somebody he'd never met about Jesus. He simply went back home, went across the street, went to where he worked and lived and said, "Let me tell you about the One who's changed my life." If you're going to be a successful and satisfied soul-winner, that's exactly how you'll do it.

Real Men Live for Jesus

Andrew never looked to live in the limelight. Andrew never preached to great crowds. He never wrote a book of the Bible. He never founded a church. He never had his own television show on the Palestinian Broadcasting Channel. As a matter of fact, after the Day of Pentecost, we really don't read anything else about Andrew in the Scripture. Whatever role he played in the early church was very much behind the scenes.

As John MacArthur said so well, "Andrew is more of a silhouette than a portrait in Scripture." Some say that he went back to fishing. Some say that he traveled around telling others about Jesus. Eusebius was an early church historian and he says that Andrew traveled up into what would be present day Russia. He was finally crucified in Achaia.

The story goes that he led the wife of a local governor to Christ, which infuriated her husband. He demanded that she renounce this new religion, but she refused. So, the governor had Andrew crucified by tying his hands and feet to what is known as a transverse cross. Tradition tells us that he lasted for two days, and as people walked by, and he hung there dying, he never stopped telling them about Jesus.

PETER

The Apostolic Spokesman

Lesson Text:

   Matthew 16:13–20

Study Texts:

The life and ministry of Peter receives considerable coverage in the New Testament. Therefore, any comprehensive study of the apostle is beyond the scope of this lesson series.

Memory Verse:

   Matthew 16:16–"And Simon Peter answered and said, Thou art the Christ, the Son of the living God."

The Study:

I. The Chronicle Of Peter:
   A. *His Name*
      The apostle has several names:
      1. *Simon*–his given name, *John 1:41*
         a. He was the "son of Jona" (barjona)–*Matthew 16:17*
         b. There are eight other Simons in the New Testament:
         Simon Zelotes (*Luke 6:15*)–an apostle, also known as Simon the Canaanite
         The Lord's step-brother (*Matthew 13:55*)
         Simon the Leper (*Matthew 26:6*)–lived in Bethany
         Simon of Cyrene (*Matthew 27:32*)– bore the Lord's cross
         Simon the Pharisee (*Luke 7:39, 40*)
         Judas Iscariot's father (*John 6:71*)
         Simon Magus (*Acts 8:9, 13, 18–24*)–the sorcerer
         Simon the Tanner (*Acts 9:43*)
   In addition to these, there are two Simeons:

    Simeon of Jerusalem (*Luke 2:25*)
    Simeon of Antioch (*Acts 13:1*)–a black pastor
  2. *Simeon*–from which the name
  Simon is derived, *Acts 15:14*
  3. *Peter*–the surname given to him by Christ, *Mark 3:16*

This name is the English form of the Greek *petros*–meaning a 'stone.' Jesus said to Peter, "thou art Peter (*"petros"*–*a stone, a pebble,*) and upon this rock (*"petra"*–a [big] rock, meaning Himself) I will build my church." Peter later made this very clear in *I Peter 2:3–8*. Christ is THE ROCK; individual members are "lively [living] stones" which are built upon the foundation (*I Corinthians 3:11; Ephesians 2:20b*) and make up a New Testament church (*I Timothy 3:15; Ephesians 2:21, 22*).

    4. *Cephas*–the Aramaic form of *Petros, John 1:42*
  B. *His Occupation*
    1. Peter was a fisherman, together with his
    brother Andrew (*Matthew 4:18*.) They were in
    partnership with James and John (*Luke 5:10*.)
    2. Peter was a man of considerable strength–*John 21:11*
  C. *His Home*
    1. Peter had a house in Bethsaida–*John 1:44; Matthew 8:14; Luke 4:38*
    2. Peter was married–*Matthew 8:14; Mark 1:30; Luke 4:38; I Corinthians 9:5*
    If Peter was the "first pope" (which he most surely was not!) he obviously wasn't celibate.

II. The Call Of Peter:

  Peter's relationship with the Lord passed through several stages:
    A. *Discipleship*–the call to follow Christ (*John 1:40–42*)
      Peter, like all the apostles, was prepared (saved and baptized) under John the Baptist's ministry, *Luke :1:17*
      Peter became a disciple of Christ's at Bathabara
    B. *Mentorship*–the call to forsake all (*Matthew 4:19; 19:27; Mark 1:17, 18*)
      This call was reiterated a second time in *Luke 5:1–11*
      During Christ's public ministry, Peter (along with the other apostles) was taught and trained by the Lord.

C. *Apostleship*–the call to the office of apostle
(*Matthew 10:2; Mark 3:16; Luke 6:14*)
D. *Leadership*–the oversight of the first Church and
beyond (*John 21:15–17; Acts 1:15; Galatians 1:18*)
E. *Statesmanship*–the great apostle to the
Jews (*Galatians 2:7; I Peter 1:1*)
1. Peter was the human writer of the two
epistles which bear his name–I & II Peter.
2. There is absolutely *no* evidence (Biblical, historical, archaeological, or otherwise) that Peter ever went to Rome. According to *I Peter 5:13*, he went to Babylon where he ministered to the Jews of the earlier Diaspora (*I Peter 1:1*.) Mesopotamia was a center of Orthodox Judaism. See: *Acts 2:9*
3. Peter's death was spoken of by Christ in *John 21:18, 19*. Tradition has him being crucified upside down. Peter became the spokesman and leader of the apostles. We often find him speaking on their behalf:
"*Master, we have toiled all the night, and have tken nothing*"–Luke 5:5
"*Behold, the fig tree which thou cursedst is withered away–Mark 11:21*
"*Behold, we have forsaken all, and followed thee; what shall we have therefore?*"–Matthew 19:27
"*Lord, to whom shall we go? thou hast the words of eternal life*"–John 6:68
"*We ought to obey God rather than men*"–Acts 5:29

III. The Character Of Peter:

If there was one word to describe the character of Peter, it would have to be "*impulsive*." Peter was the most reactive of the twelve apostles, responding sometimes without thinking and at other times with profound insight.

A. *Impetuous Peter*
The following examples of Peter either speaking or acting impulsively are matched only by the patient instruction of his Master. Christ turns our faults into faith!
1. "*Bid me come unto thee on the water*"–Matthew 14:28–31

Peter was ready to jump out of the ship and walk across the water to Christ. He began to sink after he thought about what he was doing.

Spiritual Lesson: Keep your eyes on the Lord and off the circumstances (verse 30).

2. *"Be it far from thee, Lord: this shall not be"*–Matthew 16:22; Mark 8:31–33

Peter was thinking of defending his Lord, but was actually playing the role of Satan who would do anything to keep Christ from going to the cross.

Spiritual Lesson: Christ's sole purpose in coming into this world was to die for man's sins.

3. *"Let us make here three tabernacles"*– Matthew 17:4; Mark 9: 5, 6; Luke 9:33

Peter was grouping Jesus Christ with Moses and Elijah.

Spiritual Lesson: Jesus Christ is the Son of God and God the Son (verse 5). He is not just another religious leader.

4. *"Thou shalt never wash my feet"*–John 13:8

Peter completely missed the Lord's lesson of humility and its application to man's sin.

Spiritual Lesson: There is one cleansing from sin (*Titus 3:5*)–there is continual cleansing from sins as we walk through this world (*I John 1:9*).

5. *"Yet I will never be offended"*–Matthew 26:33; Mark 14:29

Peter rejected the notion that he would ever deny Christ. Yet he did!

Spiritual Lesson: But for the grace of God, we are all subject to faltering. Peter went from self-confident boasting of his loyalty → following afar off (*Luke 22:54*) → warming himself at the enemy's fire (*Mark 14:54*) → cursing (*Matthew 26:74*.) Backsliding is always a progression downwards. *See*: Psalm 1:1–"*walketh,*" "*standeth,*" "*sitteth.*"

NOTE: In Simon Peter's defense, it should be noted that even though he followed "afar off," at least he did follow. All the other apostles (except John–*John 18:15, 16*) fled and deserted Christ (*Matthew 26:56c*)–even though they, like Peter, had pledged their total loyalty to Him (*Matthew 26:35d*.)

6. *Simon Peter smote the high priest's servant–John 18:10, 11*
Peter instinctively sought to protect Christ.

Spiritual Lesson: The sword was never shaped for the hand of the Lord's churches.

7. *"I go a fishing"–John 21:3*
We do not know why Peter led five other disciples to go fishing. It has been suggested that they were either despondent or backslidden, but they had in fact been instructed to go to Galilee, *Matthew 28:10; Mark 16:7*. Possibly Peter was discouraged over his denial of Christ, but he had already seen Christ at least *twice–John 20:25, 26*. Peter's nakedness (*verse 7*) suggests he had slipped back into his old ways.

Spiritual Lesson: Fishing for souls will be fruitless without the presence and direction of the Lord.

8. *"Lord, and what shall this man do?"–John 21:21*
Peter asked this question about young John after Christ had told him how he would die.

Spiritual Lesson: We are not to concern ourselves with what the Lord has in mind for others (except that they find and follow His will.) Our chief concern ought to be that we are faithfully doing what Christ has called us to do, *I Corinthians 4:1–5*. We could summarize these lessons Peter had to learn (sometimes the hard way) as follows: Peter came to see Who Christ really is (almighty God), and what he really was (desperately dependent upon Him!).

B. *Pious Peter*

Peter's verbal outbursts also revealed a deep awareness of divine truth. (Read the context of the following passages.)

1. *"Depart from me; for I am a sinful man"–Luke 5:8*
When we get even a glimpse of the holiness of God, we will always see ourselves as we truly are–*Isaiah 6:1–5*

2. *"To whom shall we go? Thou has the words of eternal life"–John 6:68*
There is no "Saviour #2" for us to follow. Discipleship is costly.

3. *"Thou art the Christ, the Son of the Living God"–Matthew 16:16*

Notice his understanding of who Christ is did not come via "flesh and blood" (verse 17)–spiritual understanding comes because of the new birth, *I Corinthians 2:10*.
4. *"Thou knowest that I love thee"–John 21:17*
Peter denied Christ three times–Jesus challenged the depth of his love three times.

IV. The Changing Of Peter:

God's will for our life is that we would be *conformed* (*Romans 8:29*), *informed* (*Romans 10:17*), and *transformed* (*Romans 12:2*). Peter is a wonderful example of this. Jesus took a rough fisherman and turned him into a compassionate preacher. It sometimes takes just a look from the Saviour (*Luke 22:61*). Peter preached openly and boldly on the Day of Pentecost in *Acts 2:14–40*–3,000 souls were saved. Peter preached openly at the temple in Jerusalem in *Acts 3:12–26*–5,000 men were saved. Peter stood for Christ before the Sanhedrin in *Acts 8:18–24*. Peter preached with great effect in Lydda, Saron, and Joppa in *Acts 9:35, 42*. Peter preached to Cornelius and his household, thereby bringing the Gospel to the Gentiles in *Acts 10*.

The Application:

Salvation produces a supernatural change (*II Corinthians 5:17*), and the Christian life is one of continual change. We are like a "diamond in the rough;" the Lord wants to make of us a precious jewel. *See*: *Isaiah 64:8; Jeremiah 18:1–6*. He does this primarily through His Word (*John 15:3; Ephesians 5:26, 27; Jeremiah 23:29*), but also through trials (*I Peter 1:17*.) Just as Peter was a fisherman who became a fisher of men, the Lord will take what we are and what we have, and convert it (*Luke 22:32*) into something better for His glory and His purpose.

The Lesson:

A. *Begin With An Illustration Of Change*:
  1. *A seed*–which changes into a flower
  2. *A caterpillar*–which changes into a butterfly

B. *Discuss change in a Person's Life*:
  1. *Why we need to change*
    a. Because of *what* we are–*wicked, sinful, Roans 3:23, Jeremiah 17:9*

  b. Because of *where* we are headed–
  Matthew 7:13; Revelation 21:27
 2. *The change resulting from salvation*
  a. A *change* in destiny–*John 5:24*
  b. A *change* in our nature–*II Peter 1:3, 4*
  c. A *change* in management–*I Corinthians 6:19, 20*
  d. A *change* in desire–*John 10:27; I John 2: 3–6*
  e. A *change* in affection–*Romans 5:5; I John 3:14*
  f. A *change* in understanding–*I Corinthians 2:14, 15; I John 2: 20, 27; 5:20*
 3. *The changes progressing from salvation*
 Going on to perfection (maturity) and *service–Hebrews 5:13–6:3, 9; II Peter 3:18; Philippians 3:13, 14*
 4. *Use the life of Peter to illustrate this*
 Select any incident from the study above.
 When teaching children, be sure to use visual aids–objects, pictures, flannel graph, etc.
C. *Challenge Those in Your Class To Allow the Lord to change them*
 1. Seek testimonies of how the Lord has already changed their lives.
 2. Discuss areas (*without* being too direct or personal) that need to be changed.

DISCUSSION:

- Peter failed on several occasions. How can failure in our lives be used by the Lord to produce change?

- What can we learn from the way in which Jesus dealt with failure in Peter's life?

- Think of a "faith crisis" you have personally experienced. How did God work in your life through it? *See: Luke 22:31, 32*

Peter

Sermon Title: A Faith Refined

Text: Luke 22:31–32

One of the things that make these disciples so wonderful and applicable for us to study is the fact that they were so very human. They had their faults and their failures, their strengths and their weaknesses, their victories and their defeats just like we do. Perhaps none of them was more human than the disciple we're going to study in this message, a fisherman by the name of Simon Peter. Peter's loud mouth and impulsiveness got him into a lot of trouble.

From arguing with Jesus when he was told that he would deny Him, to pulling out his sword and cutting off that servant's ear in the garden, and even rebuking Jesus Himself, Peter was his own worst enemy. But here's the thing that makes Peter so special and even so endearing to us–at the time, at the moment, he meant every single word that he said. While everybody may have been willing to stand around and twiddle their thumbs, he was going to do something even if it was wrong. And I think that there is something deep down inside a lot of us that not only admires that quality, but identifies with it as well.

As Warren Wiersbe said, "Peter was genuinely converted, unusually controversial, amazingly colorful, deeply consecrated and completely human."

The Lord used Peter to accomplish some really extraordinary things. We can make fun of him if we want to, but let's just face it, other than Jesus; he's the only person who's ever walked on water. When is the last time any of us raised somebody from the dead? Most of us have never given an invitation where 3,000 people gave their hearts to Jesus on the spot.

On the one hand he was less than ordinary, while on the other he's among the greatest Christians who have ever lived. From the moment that Jesus called Peter to lay down his nets and follow Him, until the moment that He called him home, Jesus was constantly and consistently refining his faith.

Luke 22:31–32

"And the Lord said, Simon, Simon, behold, Satan hath desired to have you, that he may sift you as wheat: But I have prayed for thee, that thy faith fail not: and when thou art converted, strengthen thy brethren."

In Peter we find the picture, not of a perfect faith, but of a progressing faith. Now, that's not what you'd think the first time that you meet him. He seems to have it all together. He seems so bold. He seems so sure. There doesn't appear to be a fearful bone in his body. On the surface there's courage, but beneath there's fear. On the surface there's confidence, but beneath there's doubt. On the surface there is strength, but beneath there is weakness.

When Jesus calls him to follow Him, he begins to be refined and strengthened and made into the powerful preacher who would one day stand up on the day of Pentecost, in front of those who crucified Jesus, and say, "You have illegally crucified the Messiah, but God has raised Him up from the dead!"

I want you to see the refining process of Peter's life and show you how Jesus made him into the mighty man of faith that we know him as today.

Peter's Initial Step of Faith

We were introduced to Peter when we studied Andrew, his brother, in the last chapter. We are told several things about Peter.

- He was a fisherman (*Matthew 4:18*).

- He had a brother named Andrew (*Matthew 4:18*).

- He was from the city of Bethsaida which means "House of Fish." (*John 1:44*).

- His father was a man by the name of Jonah (or John as we would say today). *Matthew 16:17*–Jesus called him "Simon BarJonah" = "Simon, son of Jonah" or "Simon Johnson").

- He married, and moved to a larger city on the shore of the Sea of Galilee called Capernaum (*Matthew 4:13; 8:14*).

- He had evidently been a successful businessman, partnering with James and John, the sons of Zebedee, which allowed him to have a house with a large enough courtyard to accommodate the many people who came to Jesus for healing (*Mark 1:34*).

- He met Jesus at Bethany beyond the Jordan where John the Baptist was baptizing (*Matthew 3*).
- He received a triple call from Jesus as friend, disciple, and apostle.
- He was naturally inquisitive.
- He was tenderhearted and affectionate.
- He was gifted with spiritual insight, and yet sometimes slow to understand deeper spiritual truths.
- He was self-sacrificing, yet had to struggle with selfishness.

That's a small snapshot of the man the Bible introduces to us as "Simon Peter." In *Matthew 4*, we see him as he takes his initial step of faith to follow Jesus. Jesus walks by one day and sees Peter and his brother Andrew working and says, "Hey, follow Me and I'll make you fishers of men." And, just like you would expect Peter to do, he drops his nets on the spot and follows Jesus. He probably didn't have to think about it much. He's seen Jesus before. He knew who He was. He'd seen him baptized. And when Jesus gave him the invitation, he followed without ever really looking back.

There's more faith in that one single act than a lot of people will ever exhibit. If you don't think so, just ask yourself this question: "What did I give up to follow Jesus?" Most of us, if we were honest, didn't have to give up very much. But Peter gave up everything to follow Jesus. He probably had some social standing there in Capernaum, but when he followed Jesus he lost whatever credibility he'd work to build. He's probably had some financial stability there in Capernaum, but when he followed Jesus he didn't even have a place to sleep or food to eat. He told Jesus one time, "We've left all to follow you."

That faith has to start somewhere. His mighty faith began as a miniature faith when Peter laid down his nets to follow Jesus. And even if your faith is small, it can be discovered and developed, and strengthened and refined.

What does faith mean? It means, forsaking all. I Trust Him. Don't ever forget this truth: Faith isn't like a rubber band that gets weaker the more you use it; it's like a muscle that only gets stronger through its use.

Peter's Inconsistent Walk of Faith

We see this pictured even in the account where Jesus gives him his nickname.

John 1:40–42

"*One of the two which heard John speak, and followed him, was Andrew, Simon Peter's brother. He first findeth his own brother, Simon, and saith unto him, We have found the Messiah, which is, being interpreted, the Christ. And he brought him to Jesus. And when Jesus beheld him, He said, Thou art Simon the son of Jona; thou shalt be called Cephas, which is by interpretation, A stone.*"

Jesus was looking deep into the innermost person of Peter and in His wisdom He saw that He couldn't expect more from Peter than Peter could give. However, at the same time, Jesus showed that when all of the rough edges and inconsistencies of Peter's faith had been worn down and filled in, he would have the kind of faith that Jesus could build his church upon.

Since Peter was a fisherman, I think that it's really interesting to look at the times when Peter was with Jesus around the sea and to notice how his faith fluctuated. I mean, if there was a place on this earth where a fisherman ought to be at home, you'd think that it would be on the sea. But as we'll see here in a minute, his faith evidently didn't have its sea-legs. And as you read and study scripture, there are basically five incidents that show us the scenes around the sea, but for the sake of time, let me show you the three main ones and explain what we see in these three incidents.

The *first time* is found in *Luke 5*. Here, we see Peter's lack of faith in Jesus's provision. Jesus had been teaching there along the seashore, and he stepped into Peter's boat and started giving Peter orders. Now, remember, Peter and the others had been working all night long, rowing, and hauling and casting their nets, but when the sun was beginning to rise, they hadn't caught a thing. So, this really wasn't the best time for somebody to jump into Peter's boat, even if it was Jesus, and tell him to cast out into the deep water and let down his nets for a catch.

You see, in Peter's mind, nobody knew the sea and fishing better than he did. With a bit of sarcasm in his voice, Peter said, "*Master, we have toiled all night and caught nothing, nevertheless at Your word I will let down the net."*

Don't get the idea that this was some sort of declaration of faith. Peter thought, "What does a preacher know about fishing? I mean, I'm sure he knows theology and doctrine and all of those sorts of things, but I'm a fisherman, and if I do what he tells me to do I'm going to be the laughing stock of the entire city, but I'll show him, I'll teach him a lesson about coming onto my boat and giving me orders." But Peter didn't teach Jesus a lesson, Jesus taught Peter a lesson—they caught so many fish that it almost sank their boat and they had to call for other boats to come and help them. And Peter dropped down at Jesus's feet and said, "*Depart from me, for I am a sinful man, O Lord!*"

The *second scene* is found in *Matthew 8*. Here we see Peter's lack of faith in Jesus's protection. Jesus and His disciples are on a boat out on the Sea of Galilee. Jesus is at the back of the boat asleep and a terrible storm comes up on the sea. These fearless fishermen, including Peter, are all afraid that they are going to drown, and so they go wake Jesus up and say, "*Lord, if you don't do something, we're all going to drown.*" And Jesus said, "*Why are you fearful, O you of little faith?*" Then He arose and rebuked the winds and the sea, and there was a great calm." And they said, "*Who can this be, that even the winds and the sea obey Him?*"

Can I give you something from this story that ought to be a real encouragement to you? There are two little phrases that I don't want you to forget, and they are, "*a great tempest arose*" and "*He arose.*" With the rising of every storm, there is the rising of the Savior, who alone can silence it.

The *third scene* is found in *Matthew 14*. Here we see Peter's lack of faith in Jesus's power. Jesus has sent the disciples to the other side of the sea, but when the boat gets to the middle of the sea another storm comes up. Jesus starts walking on the water to them. When they first see Him, they think it's a ghost.

Matthew 14:28–33

"*And Peter answered him and said, Lord, if it be thou, bid me come unto thee on the water. And he said, Come. And when Peter was come down out of the ship, he walked on the water, to go to Jesus. But when he saw the wind boisterous, he was afraid; and beginning to sink, he cried, saying, Lord, save me. And immediately Jesus stretched forth His hand, and caught him, and said unto him, O thou of little faith, wherefore didst thou doubt? And when they were come into the ship, the wind ceased. Then they that were in the ship came and worshipped him, saying, Of a truth thou art the Son of God."*

Peter makes the mistake we often make. In a time of crisis, he put his focus on the storm instead of the Savior. If you were to put all of Peter's highs and lows, victories and defeats into one bag, one incident, this would be it. This is Peter being Peter. One minute he's in the boat crying out in fear, the next minute he's stepping on the waves in faith. One minute he's sinking into the sea in doubt, the next he's crying out to Christ for deliverance.

In each and every one of these situations, Jesus was refining and Jesus was molding and Jesus was making Peter ready for not just a step of faith, not just a walk of faith, but a great big, giant leap of faith.

Did Peter ever blow it? Yes. There were times when he put more faith in a storm than he did in the Savior. There was a time when he worried more about what a little girl thought than what Jesus thought. There were times when he forgot who Jesus was and what Jesus could do.

In *Acts 2:14–24* let me finally show you...

Peter's Intrepid Leap of Faith

Acts 2:14–24

"But Peter, standing up with the eleven, lifted up his voice, and said unto them. Ye men of Judea, and all ye that dwell at Jerusalem, be this known unto you, and hearken to my words: For these are not drunken, as ye suppose, seeing it is but the third hour of the day. But this is that which was spoken by the prophet Joel; And it shall come to pass in the last days, saith God, I will pour out of my Spirit upon all flesh: and your sons and your daughters shall prophesy, and your young men shall see visions, and your old men shall dream dreams: And on my servants and on my handmaidens I will pour out in those days of my Spirit; and they shall prophesy: And I will shew wonders in heaven above, and signs in the earth beneath; blood, and fire, and vapour of smoke: The sun shall be turned into darkness, and the moon into blood, before that great and notable day of the Lord come: And it shall come to pass, that whosoever shall call on the name of the Lord shall be saved. Ye men of Israel, hear these words; Jesus of Nazareth, a man approved of God among you by miracles and wonders and signs, which God did by him in the midst of you, as ye yourselves also know: Him, being delivered by the determinate counsel and foreknowledge of God, ye have taken, and by wicked hands have crucified and slain: Whom God

hath raised up, having loosed the pains of death: because it was not possible that he should be holden of it."

Acts 2:38–43

"Then Peter said unto them, Repent, and be baptized every one of you in the name of Jesus Christ for the remission of sins, and ye shall receive the gift of the Holy Ghost. For the promise is unto you, and to your children, and to all that are afar off, even as many as the Lord our God shall call. And with many other words did he testify and exhort, saying, Save yourselves from this untoward generation.

Then they that gladly received his word were baptized; and the same day there were added unto them about three thousand souls. And they continued steadfastly in the apostles' doctrine and fellowship, and in breaking of bread, and in prayers. And fear came upon every soul; and many wonders and signs were done by the apostles."

Peter had been sifted. All of his fear had been replaced by faith and he fulfilled the promise that Jesus prayed for him on that day, "*But I have prayed for you, that your faith should not fail; and when you have returned to Me, strengthen your brethren.*" He did, and he continues to do so today.

THOMAS DIDYMUS

The Apostle Who had to be Sure

LESSON TEXT:

John 20:24–29

STUDY TEXTS:

Matthew 10:3; Mark 3:18; Luke 6:15; John 11:16; John 14:5, 6; John 20:24–29; John 21:1–14, Acts 1:13

MEMORY VERSE:

John 20:29–"Jesus saith unto him, Thomas, because thou has seen me, thou has believed; blessed are they that have not seen, and yet have believed."

THE STUDY:

I. The "File" On Thomas:

Apart from his name being included on the apostolic roll (in Matthew, Mark, Luke, and Acts), the only information we have concerning this apostle is found in the Gospel of John.

    A. *His Name*:

        1. *Thomas*–Hebrew for "*twin*."

        2. *Didymus*–Greek for "*double*" or "*twin*."

        These names were more than likely "nicknames," and were no doubt given because Thomas was in fact a twin.

    B. *His Reputation*:

        Thomas is usually known as "*Doubting Thomas*"–a name which has been somewhat unfairly applied. This is based on his statement in *John 20:25*–"*Except I shall see in his hands the print of the nails, and put my finger into the print of the nails, and thrust my hand into his side, I will not believe.*" In reality, the story of Thomas's doubt is a lesson on the reality and *foundation* of true *faith*. Jesus called him "*faithless*" in *John 20:27*.

II. The Faith Of Thomas:

The Gospel of John records three occasions on which Thomas speaks:

    A. *Faith When You Can't See the Light*:

        1. *John 11:16*

        2. This reveals a pessimistic side to Thomas. His statement "*let us also go, that we may die with him*" indicates he thought going to Bethany was both:

            a. *Pointless*

            "What's to be done? Lazarus is dead! It's over."

            The Lord responded to this pessimism with:

            A great truth–*verse 25*

            A great miracle–*verse 43, 44*

Times of bereavement invariably test one's faith. For believers, however, death brings sorrow but not despair–*I Thessalonians 4:13–18; I Corinthians 15:51–58*.

            b. *Dangerous*

            The disciples expressed concern over the dangers of going into Judea–*verses 7, 8*. Indeed, after the raising of Lazarus the Jewish leaders began actively plotting the death of Christ–*verses 45–53*.

        3. There are two possible interpretations of the word "him" in Thomas's statement:

            a. *The "Him" refers to Lazarus*

            This in the light of Christ's affirmation, "*Lazarus is dead*"–*verse 14*

            b. *The "Him" refers to Christ*

            If this is the case, then Thomas' statement is one expressing loyalty and devotion to the Lord–even to the point of death. When all we can see is the negative side of life, the Word of God gives us two important *faith* lessons:

- God is in control of our life–John 11:9; Matthew 6:34

- Death is not the end of life–John 11:25; Job 19:25–27

B. *Faith When You Don't Know the Way*:
 1. *John 14:5, 6*
 2. This reveals a desire for clarification on the part of Thomas. No doubt his heart was full of sorrow over the things Jesus had spoken of at the Supper, and his blurred mind had not grasped the teaching of the Lord concerning His departure. There is a progression in our Lord's teaching here:
    a. *Whither I go, ye cannot come–John 13:33b*
    b. *Whither I go, thou canst not follow me now; but thou shalt follow me afterwards–John 13:36b*
    c. *Whither I go ye know–John 14:4*
    Thomas was unable to understand this.
    See also: *John 16:5, 6, 17–19.*
 By the way, the right kinds of questions are always okay!
 3. *The Clear Answer–John 14:6*
 The answer is always *Christ*!
    a. The *way–Proverbs 4:12; 6:23; Matthew 7:13, 14*
    b. The *truth–John 8:32; 17:17; Ephesians 1:13*
    c. The *life–John 1:4; 6:35b; 10:10b*
 Note the exclusiveness of the Gospel message–*Acts 4:12; John 10:1, 9*. This is in stark contrast to today's "religious correctness."

C. *Faith When You Haven't Seen the Proof*:
 1. *John 20:24–29*
 2. Thomas was not present during the resurrection day church meeting (*John 20:1, 19–21*). Absence from the assembly is a major cause of faithlessness–*Hebrews 10:25*.
    a. He missed out on a meeting with Christ. The Lord's *special* presence is found in the *midst of His churches*, *Revelation 1:13, 20; I Corinthians 3:16, Ephesians 2:21, 22; I Timothy 3:15*.
    b. He missed out on hearing words of peace and gladness. "*Seven days without church makes one weak!*"
    c. He missed out on hearing God's plan for his life when Christ commissioned *His Church*, *verse 21*.
 3. Thomas could not believe without tangible proof. True *faith always* has *evidence* and *substance–Hebrews 11:1*.

  a. Thomas sought *tangible* physical evidence
  b. We have the *tangible* evidence of God's Word
  c. Today our *attitude* should be: "*Except I shall see it in the Bible… I will not believe.*"
  d. There is a greater blessing for believing God's Word without seeing (*Hebrews 11:27d*)–*verse 29. See also*: I Thessalonians 2:13.
  e. God has no other way than *through man believing His Word*–Luke 16:31; Hebrews 11:6.
 4. Eight days later, Jesus met with Thomas and answered all his questions.
  a. What must those eight days have been like for him?
  b. The all-knowing Christ knew what Thomas had said, *John 2:25*
  c. Thomas' statement of *faith* (*verse 28*) is a declaration of the deity of Christ. Jesus did not rebuke him for calling Him God. Why? Because He IS God! (*John 1:1–3; 5:18, 23; I Timothy 3:16; Philippians 2:6; Hebrews 1:8. cf Revelation 22:8, 9*)

The Application:

 Faith is taking God at *His Word*. It is believing the Bible and acting upon it. It is never blind. Thomas faced three crises of faith–(1) believing God when it seems foolish to do so, (2) believing God when it doesn't make sense, and (3) believing God when it cannot be demonstrated.

The Lesson:

 A. *Relate the Story of Thomas's Faithlessness*
  1. Tell the story of Jesus's resurrection and appearance to His church–*John 20:19–29*.
  2. Tell of Thomas's absence, and what this meant for him. When teaching children, be sure to use visual aids–pictures, flannel graph, etc. Use a large cardboard question mark as a visual.
 B. *Teach on Faith and Faithlessness*
  1. Carefully explain what faith is, and what its basis is.
  2. Show your students how they can increase their faith.

3. Use the story of Thomas as an example. Show how Jesus met his every doubt and concern.

4. Emphasize the memory verse. *Believing is essential to salvation, Romans 10:9, 10.*

Note: Faith and doubt are abstract terms not readily grasped by small children. Therefore it is best to focus more on the story of Thomas with younger grades.

Discussion:

- What kinds of doubts commonly keep people from trusting Christ as their Saviour?

- What are some of the faulty and false foundations underpinning people's faith today?

- Comment on the statement: "*The way to certainty is to have the right kind of doubt.*"

- What things are more important than faithful church attendance?

- In the light of *I Timothy 1:4; 6:4; and Ii Timothy 2:23*, how should we question God's Word?

Thomas

Sermon Title: The Missing Disciple

Text: John 20:19–29

Thomas is one of best known of all the disciples, but the sad thing about this disciple is that he is best known for his weakness and not his strength. He's best known for his doubt and not his faith. He's best known for where he wasn't instead of where he was.

John 20:19–24

"*Then the same day at evening, being the first day of the week, when the doors were shut where the disciples were assembled for fear of the Jews, came Jesus and stood in the midst, and saith unto them, Peace be unto you. And when he had so said, he shewed unto them his hands and his side. Then were the disciples glad, when they saw the Lord. Then said Jesus to them again, Peace be unto you: as my Father hath sent me, even so send I you. And when he had said this, he breathed on them, and saith unto them, Receive ye the Holy Ghost: Whose soever sins ye remit, they are remitted unto them; and whose soever sins ye retain, they are retained. But Thomas, one of the twelve, call Didymus, was not with them when Jesus came.*"

Here we have the strange case of the missing disciple. This is the story of the disciple who missed the very first Easter service. His name was Thomas. You see, after the crucifixion of Jesus, the Bible says that the disciples were disillusioned, they were discouraged, they were huddled behind locked doors, afraid for their very lives. And the reason for that was simple–they had just seen the Lord Jesus crucified and as far as they knew they might be next.

All of a sudden, without unlocking or even opening the door, the resurrected Jesus appeared there in that room with them. You talk about a bunch of excited disciples! The Bible says, "*Then the disciples were glad when they saw the Lord.*" What a time of excitement, what a time of encouragement as they worshipped the risen Christ.

But did you notice what the Bible says? The Bible says that there were two disciples that weren't there. Of course, one of the disciples who was missing was Judas, and we know where he was. He was already in hell. After betraying Jesus for those 30 pieces of silver, Judas went out and hung himself. He had committed suicide. So, we really didn't expect to find Judas there. But where was Thomas? Why was Thomas absent? And how can we explain the strange case of the missing disciple?

There are three things that I want you to see from this passage of Scripture.

The Cause of His Absence was Doubt

John 20:25

"The other disciples therefore said unto him, We have seen the Lord., But he said unto them, Except I shall see in his hands the print of the nails, and put my finger into the print of the nails, and thrust my hand into his side, I will not believe."

That's why he's gotten the nickname "doubting Thomas." Listen to what he said, *"Unless I see in His hands the print of the nails, and put my finger into the print of the nails, and put my hand into His side, I will not believe."* He really was a doubting disciple.

Now, let me say this. We really shouldn't be too hard on Thomas. There are a lot of other wonderful things about this man named Thomas. For example, if you'll read in *John 11:16*, you'll see where Thomas was willing to die with Jesus. Thomas wasn't some sort of superficial saint, he was a deeply dedicated disciple.

So, that leads me to ask and answer this question: can a committed Christian sometimes have doubts? Can a dedicated disciple sometimes have doubts? Of course they can. You see, every person who is a Christian can and may and will at sometime have doubt.

I'm not saying that doubts are good things. But what I am saying is that doubts are to the spirit what pain is to the body. It means that something's wrong, but it doesn't mean that you're dead, because if you were dead you wouldn't feel anything.

That's what doubt is. Doubt is faith acting up. In a strange sense, there is a bright side to doubt. You say, "Oh yeah, what's that?" Well, people don't doubt what they don't believe. They just don't believe it at all. But doubt means that you have believed, but now you don't know what you believe.

I like what Dr. Adrian Rogers said. He said, "What we need to do is doubt our doubts and believe our beliefs."

God's people can and some times will doubt. I'll give you another example. Jesus said that there was never a greater man born of a woman than John the Baptist. John the Baptist was the one who stood out there on the banks of the Jordan River and preached the Word of God. He had a rock for a pulpit, a river for a choir and the sky for an auditorium. He was the man who said when Jesus came, "*Behold the Lamb of God who takes away the sins of the World.*" That's why Jesus said, "*For I say to you, among those born of women there is not a greater prophet than John the Baptist...*" But then John the Baptist was placed in prison, and John the Baptist sent his disciples to ask Jesus, "*Are you the One we've been waiting for, or do we need to look for somebody else?*"

I love what Jesus said. Jesus didn't condemn John; as a matter of fact, Jesus was very kind and caring and sympathetic to him. John had asked Jesus an honest question and Jesus gave John an honest answer and reassured and reconfirmed his faith. Sometimes good people can have honest doubts, but God will help those who have honest doubts.

Now, what are some of the factors that cause good people to have doubt? What are some of the things that cause disciples like Thomas to doubt? Well, there are three factors that may cause you to doubt if you're not careful.

A. *The discouragement factor*: Why did Thomas doubt? He was discouraged. Why did John the Baptist doubt? He was discouraged. It's easy to see why Thomas would have been discouraged. Look in *John 20:9*, "*For as yet they did not know the Scripture, that He must rise again from the dead.*" You see, Jesus had told them over and over again that He had to die, but that after three days he would rise again. He had told them, but somehow they had never fully and finally understood it. They couldn't comprehend it. They couldn't believe it. They didn't understand the scripture–that Jesus Christ must raise from the dead.

The Bible speaks in *verse 19* of the awful fear that they had. They were afraid for their very lives. So, there was a misunderstanding, there was fear, there was tension, and it was in this kind of a situation that Thomas doubted.

Look at the kind of situation that John the Baptist was in. John the Baptist was a rugged outdoorsman. He wasn't used to being cooped up in a cold, dark, damp, dirty, and dismal prison. He must have felt trapped like a bird in a cage. You see, it's one thing to stand on the Jordan and give it. It's something else to sit in a jail cell and take it.

So, here's John the Baptist, and he's confused. He's thinking to himself, "*If Jesus can raise the dead, why can't He get me out of jail?*"

John the Baptist was like the little boy who said, "If God is God, why did He put all of the vitamins in broccoli instead of ice-cream?"

He couldn't figure out why God was doing things the way that He was. If God is God, then why doesn't He do something and get me out of this jail?

You see, John the Baptist had preached a victorious, militant Christ, but here was Jesus, meek and lowly. Maybe this is similar to your situation today. You say, "Well, pastor, you're talking about this big, great God who can do anything, but look at me. Look at the troubles I've got. My blood pressure's up and my bank account is down. I've been to the doctors and they've said that there's no hope. My kids are giving me fits. That man I work for is driving me insane. I don't know how I'm going to make ends meet." These are the kind of conditions that doubt thrives on. This is when doubt tries to sneak in—when we're discouraged.

Now, let me say this. Misunderstanding and discouragement always go together. If John the Baptist had understood that Jesus never promised to keep him out of prison, then he wouldn't have been so discouraged. If Thomas had understood that everything that took place during the crucifixion was simply the fulfillment of prophecy and solely the will of God, then maybe he wouldn't have been so discouraged.

Don't get the idea that you're too good to go through bad times. Hey, let me tell you something. The same God that didn't keep John from the jail cell; the same God that didn't keep the three Hebrew children out of the fiery furnace; the same God that didn't keep Daniel out of the lion's den; the same God that didn't keep David out of the valley of the shadow of death is not going to pamper you. Listen, if you think that just because you're a Christian, you're not going to have any troubles or trials or tribulations, you're wrong. Jesus said, "*In this world you will have tribulation.*" If you don't have it, then Jesus is wrong, because He said that you were going to have it.

Doubt and discouragement go together. Thomas was discouraged and he misunderstood and as a result he doubted. Christianity is not the subtraction of problems from life. It is the addition of power to meet those problems. God knows what He's doing. God is in the business of making all things work together for good to those who love the Lord and who are the called according to His purpose.

B. *The disobedience factor.* I have the idea that Thomas was being disobedient when He wasn't in the worship service with those other disciples. I say that because one of the precepts of scripture is that God's people are not supposed to forsake the assembling of themselves together.

If you're having trouble with doubt, then try repentance. You see, there is an order in the Bible that is never, ever broken and here it is–repentance and faith, repentance and faith, repentance and faith. Not faith and repentance, it's always repentance and faith. That's why I say to you if you're having trouble with your faith, try repentance. Repentance always comes first.

C. *There is the demonic factor.* Don't you know that Satan will fling fiery darts of doubt your way? Don't you know that Satan will do anything and everything that he can in order to get you to doubt? Don't ever discount a demon of doubt. You say, "Pastor, are you saying that you believe that there are literal demons that I'll have to deal with?" That's exactly what I'm saying, and one of the chief demons is the demon of doubt.

Don't you know that the devil hates the idea of the resurrection? Don't you know that the devil has aimed all of the big guns of hell at the fact of the resurrection? Do you know why that is? It's because the demons in hell know what would happen if you and I ever really came to the conclusion that Jesus is just as alive today as He was two thousand years ago.

All heaven would break loose if we were to really believe in the power of His resurrection. These are some factors that I'm sure that old Thomas had to deal with. There was the discouragement factor. There was the disobedience factor. And there was the demonic factor. So, that was the cause of Thomas's absence.

The Cost of His Absence

What did it really cost when this disciple wasn't where he was supposed to be? What happens when you're not in the House of God?

Now, a lot of times you'll hear somebody say something like this: "Well, you don't have to go to church to be a good Christian." Sounds good, but there's just one thing wrong with that statement: it's not true.

Oh, I know that there are some folks who can't come for one reason or another, but I'm talking about those folks who can come but don't come. I'm talking about those people who are willfully, deliberately missing church. What did it cost Thomas when he missed that first Easter service?

A. *It cost his influence.* Don't forget that there were two who were absent that evening–Judas and Thomas. Do you see what kind of a crowd that he put himself in? Do you see how he associated himself? Those were the only two who were absent and as far as the other disciples could know, Thomas and Judas could have been in cahoots.

Don't you realize that when you miss coming to church that you're casting a vote with the devil's crowd and against the House of God? Don't you realize that when you stay away from church that you're casting a vote to close its doors? How are you going to vote on Sunday night? How are you going to vote Wednesday night? You say, "Well, this is a Baptist church and you know, pastor, majority rules." I don't believe that, because if the majority got their way we wouldn't have church on Sunday night or Wednesday night. God help us if the majority gets to have their way. Thank God for those believers who are faithful to the House of God.

So, his influence suffered. You see, you don't just come to church for what you can get, you ought to come to church for what you can give.

I heard about a little confederate granny during the Civil War who looked out her kitchen window and saw some Yankee soldiers coming across the field. Well, she grabbed a poker from the fire place and started out across that yard waving that poker and screaming at the top of her lungs. Her grandchildren caught her and said, "Granny, what in the world are you doing? You can't do anything against all of those soldiers with their guns and swords." She said, "I can show them what side I'm on."

Let me tell you something. When you come to church, if you don't do anything else, when you put your clothes on and bring your family and your Bible to church, if you don't do anything else, you're letting a lost, Jesus hating world know whose side you're on.

B. *It cost his church.* You see, not only did his influence suffer, but his church suffered. Your local church needs you. You need to be in God's House on God's day. The Bible says that you're *not to forsake the assembling of yourselves together as the manner of some is, but so much the more as you see the day approaching.*

C. *It cost his faith.* He was in bad enough shape already without missing church. I mean, if there ever was a man who needed to be in church, he needed to be in church. If he's been there he would have met the Lord Jesus because even though Thomas didn't show up, Jesus did. Have you ever stopped to realize that just because you don't show up doesn't mean that Jesus doesn't show up either? Aren't you glad that Jesus said, *"For where two or three are gathered together in My name, I am there in the midst of them."*

You say, "Well, I stay home and watch that preacher on TV and that's my church." No, it's not. Listen, no television service can ever replace the gathering together of God's people in one place to worship Him. Jesus said, *"For where two or three are gathered together in My name, I am there in the midst of them."*

The Bible doesn't teach a lone-ranger Christianity. If you're sick, disabled or shut-in, that's one thing, but if you don't have enough faith to get you to church I wonder if you've got enough faith to get you to Heaven.

D. *It cost his joy.* The Bible says in verse 20, *"Then the disciples were glad when they saw the Lord."* You know, I hate to miss church. And really the Lord's blessed me. In my 23 years as a pastor, I've only missed three Sunday mornings due to sickness. I hate to miss church. Wouldn't you hate to have been Thomas? He missed that first service when Jesus showed up and the disciples came running to him and said, *"We've seen the Lord."* Don't you feel sorry for Thomas? The Bible says, *"Then the disciples were glad when they saw the Lord."* But he wasn't there. He missed it. It cost him his joy.

The Cure for His Absence

What happened to Thomas? Well, the first thing is that he came in contact with the disciples who had seen Jesus.

A. *The testimony of Spirit-filled believers.*
John 20:24–25

"But Thomas, one of the twelve, called Didymus, was not with them when Jesus came. The other disciples therefore said unto him, We have seen the Lord. But he said unto them, Except I shall see in his hands the print of the

nails, and put my finger into the print of the nails, and thrust my hand into his side, I will not believe."

They had a visitation program. Somebody was absent and they went after him. Did you notice what they did? Did you notice what they said? They found Thomas and they told him all of the exciting things that had happened in the service. They didn't say, "O, Thomas, you should have been there. Mary Magdalene wore the prettiest dress you've ever seen." That isn't what they said. They didn't say, "You sure picked the right day to miss. Jesus preached for over an hour. I didn't think He'd ever get done, and the Methodists beat us to the buffet down at the restaurant." That isn't what they said. They were excited, and they said as they came out of that room, filled with the Holy Spirit, "*Thomas, we have seen the Lord.*" There was something about their testimony that set him on fire.

B. *The testimony of the facts.*

John 20:26–28

"*And after eight days again his disciples were within, and Thomas with them: then came Jesus, the doors being shut, and stood in the midst, and said, Peace be unto you. Then saith he to Thomas, reach hither thy finger, and behold my hands; and reach hither thy hand, and thrust it into my side: and be not faithless, but believing. And Thomas answered and said unto him, My Lord and my God.*"

Thomas was convinced because not only did he have the testimony of his friends, but he had the testimony of the facts. He could see the nail prints in Jesus's hands with his own eyes.

Now, of course, we don't have the ability or the opportunity to see the physical body of Jesus like Thomas did, but does that mean that we don't have any facts? No. There are facts today that can be seen and studied. The Bible says that after the resurrection Jesus showed Himself alive by many infallible proofs.

Now, if you choose not to believe, that's your business, but it will not be because there are no facts to believe. It will not be because you cannot believe. There is more proof that Jesus Christ rose from the dead than there is that a man named Julius Caesar ever lived. The Bible says that *He showed Himself alive by many infallible proofs.*

C. *The testimony of Scripture.*

John 20:29–31

"*Jesus saith unto him, Thomas, because thou hast seen me, thou hast believed: blessed are they that have not seen, and yet have believed. And many other signs truly did Jesus in the presence of his disciples, which are not written in this book: But these are written, that ye might believe that Jesus is the Christ, the Son of God; and that believing ye might have life through his name."*

Jesus said, "I'm going to give you something better than signs and wonders. I'm going to give you something better than even seeing me with your physical eyes." He said, "I'm going to give you my Word." And God has given us the Bible to prove the supernatural resurrection of Jesus Christ.

You say, "Well, I just don't know if I can believe the Bible." Well, Jesus talked about you. He said in *Luke 16:31*, *"But he said to him, 'If they do not hear Moses and the prophets, neither will they be persuaded though one rise from the dead."*

I'm telling you, if you won't believe the Bible, you wouldn't be persuaded even if you met the resurrected Jesus.

NATHANAEL BARTHOLOMEW

The Skeptical Apostle

LESSON TEXT:

John 1:43–51

STUDY TEXTS:

Matthew 10:3; Mark 3:18; Luke 6:14; John 1:43–51; John 21:2; Acts 1:13

MEMORY VERSE:

John 1:49–"Nathanael answered and said unto him, Rabbi, thou art the Son of God; thou art the King of Israel."

THE STUDY:

I. Identifying Nathanael:

Nathanael (who is *not* mentioned in any of the apostolic lists) is considered to be the same person as Bartholomew (who is mentioned in every list) (1) by process of elimination, and (2) because Bartholomew's name is paired with Philip's in the Gospel lists. It was Philip who introduced the Lord Jesus Christ to Nathanael.

    A. *His Name*:

        1. *Nathanael* = *"gift of God."*

        2. *Bartholomew* (a surname) = *"son of Tolmai."*

    B. *His Birthplace*:

From *John 21:2*, we learn that Nathanael was from Cana. This was a village about 8 miles NNE of Nazareth. It was the place where Jesus did His first miracle (*John 2:1–11*).

    C. *His Apostleship*:

Nathanael *was* in Galilee *when* he met the Lord Jesus Christ for the first time.

        1. *Nathanael's Friend–John 1:45*

            a. Philip sought him–a 20 mile journey from Bethsaida to Cana.

b. Philip told him the *news*–notice his appeal to the Word of God. (Philip was the "*show me*" apostle.)

2. *Nathanael's Frown–John 1:45*

It seems Nazareth had a reputation as *low class town*. Evidently, its residents were aloof because of its strategic location–even to the point of throwing their trash onto the main street to discourage visitors.

3. *Nathanael's Fig Tree–John 1:48*

This was a place of peace and meditation–*I Kings 4:25; Micah 4:4, Zechariah 3:10*

Nathanael was a thinking man. He was no doubt patiently awaiting the arrival of the Messiah after hearing (and responding to) the preaching of John the Baptist.

4. *Nathanael's Finding–John 1:47, 49*

    a. He found out that Jesus already knew all about him, *verse 47*.

    b. He affirmed Who Jesus was, *verse 49*. This according to the law and the prophets (*Isaiah 9:6, 7*).

    The Son of God–a declaration of His deity

    The King of Israel–a declaration of His sovereignty.

5. *Nathanael's Future–John 1:50, 51*

Our Lord's prophecy here refers to His second coming and the judgment of the nations prior to the establishment of His millennial kingdom.

See: *Matthew 19:27, 28; 25:31–34*.

II. Analyzing Nathanael:

We note two things about Nathanael, based on the Lord's analysis of him:

    A. *He Was An "Israelite Indeed."*

Nathanael was a saved man–*Romans 9:6b; 11:5*. He was also a man who was earnestly searching the scriptures (*John 5:39*). Philip's announcement to him was: "*We have found him, of whom Moses in the law, and the prophets, did write…*" This indicates both he and Philip were looking.

1. *Moses prophesied of Christ*–e.g., *Genesis 3:15; 49:10; Numbers 24:17, Deuteronomy 18:15, 18*

  2. *The Prophets spoke of Christ*–e.g., *Isaiah 7:14; 9:6, 7; 53:3–10; Micah 5:1-4; etc.*
 B. *He was A Man Without Guile*
  This speaks of his sincerity. He was a plain speaker–not given to deception or double-speak. Remember the first Israel (Jacob) was a supplanter (full of guile.)
   See: *Psalm 32:2*
  Nathanael's response to Philip's announcement reveals his skeptical nature.
  Perhaps it was based on:
  1. *Prejudice*–i.e., Nazareth's reputation
   Prejudice means 'pre-judging." It is judging without any factual basis.
    See:*John 7:24*
   Note: One's reputation is important, if not for this very reason!
  2. *Ignorance*
   Perhaps Nathanael was ignorant of what the grace of God could do–anywhere, any time, and in any one (even in Nazareth!)
  3. *Incomplete knowledge*
   Philip's description of Christ was incomplete. He spoke of:
   a. *Jesus of Nazareth*–yet Nathanael, a serious student of the Bible, surely knew the Messiah was to be born in Bethlehem. Perhaps he missed reading that He would also come from Galilee–*Isaiah 9:1, 2; Matthew 4:13–16.*
   b. *The son of Joseph*–yet Joseph was not the biological father of Jesus. He had no father save God! This reference to Jesus may indicate that Philip and Nathanael knew the Lord from His years growing up in Nazareth. Facts are always so important.

III. Satisfying Nathanael:
 A. *From the Human Side*–"*come and see!*"
  This is always the answer to the skeptic.
  Check it out for yourself.

See: *Psalm 34:8a; John 4:29; Acts 17:11*

B. *From the Divine Side*

The Lord convinced Nathanael by proving He was indeed the One spoken of in the law and the Prophets. How? By showing His *omniscience* (all-knowingness.) This is an attribute of God–*Psalm 139:1–4; Proverbs 15:3; II Chronicles 16:9; Job 37:16; Acts 15:18; Isaiah 49:9, 10; Romans 11:33; I John 3:20*

1. He knew his Character–*John 1:47*
2. He knew his Actions–*John 1:48*
3. He knew his Future–*John 1:50, 51*

The fact is, Christ knows all about us–and still loves us! *See*: *John 2:24, 25; 4:16–19.*

THE APPLICATION:

Our judgments and life's decisions must be based squarely upon the facts of the Word of God–not on prejudice or hearsay. Skepticism must always be answered by the Word of God. The Lord always honors an honest seeker. *See*: *Proverbs 8:17; Matthew 7:7; Acts 10:1–5&c.* (He will aid the sincere seeker–He will not aid the cynical skeptic.)

THE LESSON:

A. *The Story of Nathanael Bartholomew*
1. Show that Nathanael is listed among the apostles.
2. Tell the story of Nathanael under the fig tree. When teaching children, be sure to use visual aids–pictures flannel graph, etc.

B. *Skepticism & Sincerity*
1. What does it take to believe? Feelings, or facts?
2. Teach how our prejudices can keep us from the truth.

DISCUSSION:

- Jesus saw Nathanael under the *fig* tree - probably during a time of prayer and private devotion. What does He see under *your* fig tree?

- How does prejudice affect things such as:
  » Christian fellowship?
  » Missions?

Nathanael

Title: The Disciple Who Lost a Prejudice and Found the Savior

Text: John 1:45–51

> "Philip findeth Nathanael, and saith unto him, We have found him, of whom Moses in the law, and the prophets, did write, Jesus of Nazareth, the son of Joseph. And Nathanael said unto him, Can there any good thing come out of Nazareth? Philip saith unto him, Come and see. Jesus saw Nathanael coming to him, and saith of him, Behold an Israelite indeed, in whom is no guile! Nathanael saith unto him, Whence knowest thou me? Jesus answered and said unto him, Before that Philip called thee, when thou wast under the fig tree, I saw thee. Nathanael answered and saith unto him, Rabbi, thou art the Son of God; thou art the King of Israel. Jesus answered and said unto him, Because I said unto thee, I saw thee under the fig tree, believest thou? thou shalt see greater things than these. And he saith unto him, Verily, verily I say unto you, Hereafter ye shall see heaven open, and the angels of God ascending and descending upon the Son of man."

One of the most famous sports bloopers ever happened in the 1930 Rose Bowl. You've probably seen a clip of it at one time or the other. Roy Reigle recovered a fumble. He was playing for the University of Southern California. This was his big moment. There was the ball. He picked it up and made a dazzling and an amazing run and scored a touchdown. There was only one problem. He ran the wrong way and he scored it for the wrong team. Roy was sincere. He was as sincere as he could be, but he was sincerely wrong.

Well, in *John 1* we have the story of a sincere man, but just like Roy Reigle, it's the story of a man who was sincerely wrong. Here was a man who the Bible shows us had a big prejudice, but who at the same time had no deceit. You see, he was confused, he was upset, his mind was distorted—but he liked it that way. He was like a lot of people who live today. They're good people who have wrong ideas. They're sincere, but they're sincerely wrong. His name was Nathanael.

Now, as you read through the Gospels, what you'll find is that

Matthew, Mark and Luke call him Bartholomew," while John calls him "Nathanael." Actually "Bartholomew" was his last name, and his first name was "Nathanael," so his full name was really "Nathanael Bartholomew."

There are several things that I want you to notice about this disciple who lost a prejudice and found the Savior.

HIS DIVINE CONFRONTATION

He had a confrontation with Jesus. He was confronted with Jesus by Philip. Now, if you'll remember that when we studied Philip we found that Philip was the level-headed man. He was the facts and figures fellow. He was the show-me disciple. He had to figure things out and know in his own mind that Jesus was who He claimed to be. So, Philip studied the scriptures and as a result he came to the conclusion that Jesus Christ was indeed the Messiah. And Philip got so excited about it that he found Nathanael and told him!

Now, when we studied about Philip, I mentioned some of the prophecies about the Lord Jesus Christ that are found in the Bible, but I really didn't give them to you in great detail. So, let me take just a moment and share with you some of these Old Testament Scriptures, because I believe that this will be a real encouragement to you just as they were for Philip.

What does the Old Testament prophecy about the Lord Jesus Christ?

- He was to be the seed of the woman: *Genesis 3:15*
- He was to be the seed of Abraham: *Genesis 22:18*
- He was to be the seed of David: *Jeremiah 23:5*
- He was to be of the tribe of Judah: *Genesis 49:10*
- The time of his coming was prophesied in *Daniel 9:24–25*
- He would be born of a virgin: *Isaiah 7:14*
- The place where He would be born: *Micah 5:2*
- His forerunner, John the Baptist: *Malachi 3:1*
- He would be betrayed by a friend: *Psalm 41:9*
- His triumphal entry into Jerusalem: *Zechariah 9:9*
- He would be sold for 30 pieces of silver: *Zechariah 11:12*

- He would die by crucifixion: *Psalm 22 and Isaiah 53*
- He would be raised from the dead: *Psalm 16:10*

All of these scriptures prophesied and predicted the Lord Jesus Christ. Not all of them had been fulfilled when Philip got so excited that he wanted to go tell Nathanael, but just think of the ones that had been.

Like Dr. Adrian Rogers called them, these prophecies were "ever converging, concentric circles that were closing in on the person of Christ." For example, think about it.

- God had predicted which race the Messiah would come from–the human race, the seed of the woman.
- God went on and prophesied what division of that race the Messiah would come from–He'd be a descendent of Seth.
- God went on and prophesied what nation of that division of that race the Messiah would come from–the Jewish nation, a descendant of Abraham.
- The Lord went on and prophesied what tribe of that nation of that division of that race that the Messiah would come from–the tribe of Judah.
- God went on and prophesied what family of that tribe of that nation of that division of that race the messiah would come from–the family of David.
- God went on and prophesied what person of that family of that tribe of that race of that division of that race the Messiah would come from–the virgin.
- He even prophesied what place and what tie the Messiah would be born–Bethlehem Ephrata.

Can't you see it as God's great telescope comes into focus? Isn't it absolutely amazing how the Bible takes all of these scriptures and closes in on every side, until finally it centers upon one person–Jesus Christ of Nazareth?

That's one of the ways that Philip knew that Jesus was the Messiah. He ran to tell Nathanael and Nathanael had a divine confrontation; he was confronted with the person of the Lord Jesus Christ.

His Disappointing Confusion

You see, not only was he confronted with Jesus, He was confused about Jesus.

Now, what was the confusion that was in Nathanael's mind? Well, as you'll notice there in verse 46, Nathanael had a prejudice. He didn't like the Nazarenes. He was prejudiced against the Nazarenes, and he had made up his mind that nothing good could come out of Nazareth, and since Jesus was from Nazareth, He was automatically bad.

This wasn't something that was unique to Nathanael. As a matter of fact, this was a commonly held thought in those days because most people kind of looked down their noses at the Nazarenes.

Now, let me ask you a question. What caused Nathanael's prejudice? Well, the thing that really caused his prejudice was his ignorance. You see, the mother of prejudice is ignorance and the child of ignorance is prejudice. Remember that. If Nathanael had known his Bible, he would have known that the Messiah would come from Nazareth because the Bible says in *Matthew 2:23*, *"And he came and dwelt in a city called Nazareth, that it might be fulfilled which was spoken by the prophets, "he shall be called a Nazarene."* You see, Nathanael's ignorance caused his prejudice. If he'd known his Bible, he wouldn't have had the prejudice that he had.

Prejudice comes when we make certain conclusions and assumptions without having all of the facts. Nathanael's problem was his prejudice and his prejudice was rooted in ignorance.

Nathanael almost missed finding Jesus because he had a preconceived idea—*"Can anything good come out of Nazareth"*

His Dynamic Conversion

You see, not only was he confronted with Jesus and confused about Jesus, he was converted to Jesus. How did he come to the Lord Jesus Christ? The same way we all have to come to the Lord. First of all, you're going to have to come…

A. *Humbly*
Matthew 11:25–26

"At that time Jesus answered and said, I thank thee, O Father, Lord of heaven and earth, because thou has hid these things from the wise and prudent, and hast revealed them unto babes. Even so, Father: for so it seemed good in thy sight."

Do you know what that means? That means that you're going to have to come with a child-like mind. "*God has hidden these things from the wise and the prudent.*" If you want to know the truth about Jesus, you're going to have to put away your formulas and your figures, you're hang-ups and your haughty spirit, because the Bible says that if you come to God that way, he'll hide these things from you and reveal them to those who come with a child-like faith. You're going to have to come humbly if you come.

You know why that is? It is because a little child is teachable. I know some adults who are so proud and so fixed in their mind that God Himself couldn't get through to them. You see, a child is teachable. He's humble.

B. *Openly*

You've got to really want to know. Here's God's promise to the prophet Jeremiah in *Jeremiah 29:13*, "… *you will seek Me and find Me, when you search for Me with all your heart.*" If you want to know, you can know. God says, "*You can seek for me, and you can find me when you come with an open heart.*" Now, if you come with a divided heart, if you come with mixed motives, if you come looking for some sort of ammunition to back up your argument, you're not going to find the truth.

On an office wall there was a poster that read, "My mind is made up, don't confuse me with the facts." That's the way that some folks are. They don't want to know the truth about Jesus. They don't come openly and honestly looking for the truth.

That's the way that some people are. Rather than trying to find the truth and discover a principle, they're defending a prejudice. They don't want the condition of their hearts exposed. That's why they fight. They don't really want to know the truth.

C. *Diligently*

Proverbs 2:3–5

"*Yea, if thou criest after knowledge, and liftest up they voice for understanding; If thou seekest her as silver, and searchest for her as for hid treasures; Then shalt thou understand the fear of the Lord, and find the knowledge of God.*"

God is saying that we need to get as interested in knowing Him as we are in earning money. There is a diligence involved in coming to be saved.

D. *Submissively*

You see, truth isn't something that you learn so that you can say "that's interesting" and then put it aside and not do anything with it. Truth is more than just interesting, it's unsettling. Not only must you be willing to revise your ideas, you must be willing to reform your life. What I'm saying is this–if you want to know the truth about God you must be willing to do the will of God. Does that make sense?

Before you come, you've got to surrender your will.

Nathanael was dynamically converted because he came humbly, he came openly, he came diligently and he came submissively. But he came. Philip said to Nathanael, "*Nathanael, come and see.*" Nathanael came, he saw and he believed.

What was Nathanael doing under that fig tree? I don't think he was doing anything wrong. I think he was probably studying the Bible. You see, in that climate this was kind of like their air-conditioning. Almost every home would have a fig tree outside the front door and people would get out there in the shade and sit underneath that fig tree. I believe that Nathanael was studying the Scriptures. I believe that he wanted to know the truth. Of course, the Lord Jesus Christ by His omniscience knew all about Nathanael. So, Nathanael said, "O, He knows my race. O, He knows my heart. O, He knows my past. He knows all about me. How could He know all of these things?" And that's all it took to convince Nathanael. Jesus just started with him where he was in order to get him to where He wanted him to be. And Jesus will do the same with you today. If you'll just be honest, Jesus Christ will start with you where you are and he will give you whatever is necessary in order to lead you to the truth.

His Direct Confession

Look back at *John 1:49*. Nathanael is convinced, and so he said to Him, "*Rabbi, You are the Son of God! You are the King of Israel!*" What did he call Jesus? He called Him *master, mediator and messiah.* The word "*Rabbi*" means master. "Son of God" means mediator. "The King of Israel" means messiah. That was his dynamic confession.

Are you willing to make that confession? Are you willing to confess the Lord Jesus Christ as your master? If you are, He will save you. I'll guarantee you, based on the authority of the Bible "*that if you confess with your mouth the Lord Jesus and believe in your heart that God has raised Him from the dead, you will be saved.*" It's not enough to say it with your lips; you've got to mean it with your life.

Years ago, there was a man out in California that was known as "The Human Fly." He climbed up buildings and bridges without a rope or a net, and on this particular day he was climbing up a very tall department store as part of a publicity stunt. Thousands were there to watch him. He started up the side of that building, holding on to this corner and that ledge. He's get a toe in here or a finger in there, up and up he climbed. Four stories. Five stories. Six stories. Finally, when he was almost to the top, he seemed to run out of any place to get a toe or a finger in order to make it to the top. He looked over and there seemed to be a dark piece of the building that stuck out a little bit, just out of the reach of his fingers. So, he figured that he could jump just a bit and catch it and finish his climb. He jumped toward what he thought was a dark piece of stone, but all of a sudden he plummeted to the ground. When they found his crushed body, they pried open his hand and there they found that he had reached for and grabbed a spider web. It was just a crusted spider web. That's what he had in his hand.

There are folks who are trying to climb to Heaven and they're putting their trust in nothing any stronger than a crusty spider web when they ought to be putting their trust in the Rock of Ages, Jesus Christ.

Jesus said, "*I am the way, the truth, and the life, no one comes to the Father except through me.*"

JAMES, THE SON OF ALPHAEUS

James the Less

LESSON TEXT:

Matthew 10:3

STUDY TEXTS:

Matthew 10:3; Mark 3:18; Mark 15:40; Luke 6;15; Acts 1:13

MEMORY VERSE:

John 3:30–"He must increase, but I must decrease."

THE STUDY:

I. The Unknown Apostle:

James the son of Alphaeus is the least-known of all the apostles. His name only occurs in the apostolic lists. No particular word or deed is ascribed to him.

    A. *His Names*:

        1. There are *three* Jameses mentioned in the *New* Testament:

            a. James, the son of Zebedee–an apostle

            b. James, the Lord's step-brother–*Matthew 13:55*

            c. James, the son of Alphaeus

        2. His "*nickname*" was James the LESS.

            a. The word "less" is translated from the Greek word '*mikros*' meaning "small."

            b. James may have been thus-called because of his stature. i.e., He was short.

            c. James may have been called this because of his position. He wasn't as prominent among the apostles as was James the son of Zebedee.

    B. *His Family*:

        By comparing *Matthew 27:56; Mark 15:40 and John 19:25*, we can determine that:

1. His mother's name was Mary
2. His father's name was both Cleophas (Hebrew) and Alphaeus (Greek.)
> *Note*: An Alphaeus was the father of the apostle Matthew (*Mark 2:14*.) This could mean James was the brother of Matthew, although this is not conclusive.
> *Note*: A Cleophas was one of the two disciples whom Jesus met on the road to Emmaus–*Luke 24:13–18*
3. He had brothers named Judas and Joses.

II. The Self-Reduction Principle:

A. *The Christian Motto*: John 3:30–"He must increase, but I must decrease."
1. John the Baptist gave way to Christ as he fulfilled his course (his calling and ministry)–*Acts 13:25*.
2. There needs to be more and more of Christ; less and less of me–*Colossians 1:18*.
3. This is often contrary to the way of man–*Proverbs 20:6; Romans 12:3*.

B. *Greater Than John*: Matthew 11:11–"Verily I say unto you, Among them that are born of women there hath not risen a greater than John the Baptist: notwithstanding he that is least ["micros"] in the kingdom of heaven is greater than he."

C. *God Uses Little Things*:
Popularity and position have little to do with serving the Lord acceptably.
1. God used Gideon–*Judges 6:15*
2. God used Saul–*I Samuel 9:21*
3. God uses small beginnings–*Zechariah 4:10a*
4. God used Bethlehem–*Matthew 2:6*
5. God is concerned with the smallest details–*Luke 16:10*
6. God assigns important tasks to the most insignificant church members–*I Corinthians 6:4*

D. *God Used James The Less*:
Although he is the least known of all the apostles, he was nonetheless still an apostle of the Lamb.
1. He personally experienced the great power of God–*Luke 9:1*

2. He personally witnessed the greatest event in human history–*I Corinthians 15:7*
3. He personally received the great commandments of the Lord–*Acts 1:2*
4. He was personally involved in the great moving of God on the Day of Pentecost and beyond–*Acts 2:14, 37; 4:33*
5. He was personally involved in the great church at Jerusalem–*Acts 2:42, 43*
6. He personally suffered great persecution–*Acts 5:18, 29, 40, 41*
7. He will one day rejoice over the great destruction of Babylon–*Revelation 18:20*
8. His name will forever be recorded in the foundations of the great City of God–*Revelation 21:14*

Not bad for an "unknown," eh?

THE APPLICATION:

We are never too small, we are never too insignificant, that we cannot be used of God. God is not concerned with our ability–just our availability!

Little is much, when God is in it.
Labor not for wealth of fame.
There's a crown, and you can win it–
If you'll go in Jesus' Name

THE LESSON:

A. *Review*:

Use this lesson to review the entire study on the twelve apostles.
1. Pick out one striking characteristic of each man
2. Write that characteristic on a board. You could play a game with those in your class–match the characteristic with the name. Use visual aids.

B. *James The Less*:

Teach about James the Less
1. Explain the difference between greatness and fame
2. Show how each one can be great in the sight of God

3. Point out the right motive–to magnify Christ.

DISCUSSION:

- How does the testimony of James the Less epitomize the lives of all the apostles?
- What lessons have you learned through the study of the twelve apostles?

James the Less

Title: Little Is Much When God Is In It

Text: Luke 6:15

Matthew and Thomas, James the son of Alphaeus, and Simon called Zelotes

Mark 15:40

"There were also women looking on afar off: among whom was Mary Magdalene, and Mary the mother of James the less and of Joses, and Salome;"

We have been studying about the 12 men whom Jesus called to come after Him and become His disciples. Now, sometimes they were called disciples and sometimes they were called apostles. The word "disciple" means "learner" and the word "apostle" means "one who is sent forth." And that's what they were. They followed Jesus for about three-and-a-half years. Then, at the end of His ministry here on earth He sent them forth to teach others as they had been taught. That's why Jesus said in

Matthew 28:19–20

"Go ye therefore, and teach all nations, baptizing them in the name of the Father, and of the Son, and of the Holy Ghost: Teaching them to observe all things whatsoever I have commanded you: and, lo, I am with you always, even unto the end of the world. Amen."

By the way, that's still the way that it's supposed to work today. There is a time when you need to learn, but there comes a time when you need to go out and disciple others.

Jesus went out and called forth those that nobody else would have wanted. And yet, Jesus called them and Jesus poured His life into them. He then sent them out to totally transform this world. Let me show you why?

I Corinthians 1:27–29

"But God hath chosen the foolish things of the world to confound the wise; and God hath chosen the weak things of the world to confound the things which are mighty; And base things of the world, and things which are despised, hath

God chosen, yea, and things which are not, to bring to nought things that are: That no flesh should glory in his presence."

You see, from that day until now, when you look at what Jesus did in these men and through these men, there's only one thing that you can say, "It's all God." I mean, it's not ability, personality, heredity, or popularity–it's all God. And perhaps that was not truer in the life of any of the other disciples than in the man who we are going to be studying in this message.

We don't know much about this disciple, other than what the above verses tell us. We know that he was the son of a man by the name of Alphaeus and a woman by the name of Mary. And since that's true, most likely he was the brother of the disciple, Matthew and some well-known believer named Joseph. That's really all that we know about his background or family. As a matter of fact, the only real insight that we get into who he was as an individual comes from the title or the nickname that he's given in *Mark 15:40* where he's called "*James the less.*"

Now, just so you don't get this James mixed up with al of the other Jameses in the Bible, let me tell you who he wasn't.

This wasn't "James, the son of Zebedee" the brother of John and one of the "Sons of Thunder."

This wasn't "James, the half-brother of Jesus."

This wasn't "James, the father of Judas–not Iscariot" as the Bible calls him.

This was "James, the son of Alphaeus" who was known as "James the less." And really, you know, there has never been a title given that was probably more accurate about a man's person or position that this telling title that was given to this man by the name of James.

I believe that there are a few really encouraging things that we discover about this man by the name of James.

The Inherent Meaning of His Name

Now, what does the word "less" mean? I know that seems like a simple question, but there's a lot rolled up in this little word. You see, the word "less" is really the Greek word *micros*. It simply means "little" or technically, "very little."

Now, we use this little word all the time. In school you may have studied "microbiology." You may have even used a "microscope." If you work in a machine shop or a garage you may use a "micrometer." If you're into finances, you've probably talked about "microeconomics."

Literally, this word is the "diminutive" of something. For example, in *Mark 9:42* this word is used to mean...

A. *Younger.* Jesus said, "*But whoever causes one of these little ones who believe in me to stumble, it would be better for him if a millstone were hung around his neck, and he were thrown into the sea.*"

In *Matthew 13:31–32* this word is used to mean...

B. *Smaller.* Jesus said, "*The kingdom of heaven is like a mustard seed, which a man took and sowed in his field, "which indeed is the least of all the seeds; but when it is grown it is greater than the herbs and becomes a tree, so that the birds of the air come and nest in its branches.*"

In *Revelation 3:8* this word is used to mean...

C. *Weaker.* The glorified Lord said, "*I know your works. See, I have set before you an open door, and no one can shut it; for you have a little strength, have kept My word, and have not denied My name.*"

And in *Matthew 18:2–3* it's used to describe those who have less...

D. *Influence or status.* "*Then Jesus called a little child to Him, set him in the midst of them, and said, "Assuredly, I say to you, unless you are converted and become as little children, you will by no means enter the kingdom of heaven.*" Think about it, what has less influence, less status than a little child. They can't determine when they go to bed, what they wear to school, what they eat for dinner, or anything.

So, that's what the word means. It means, younger, smaller, weaker or a person who has little influence or status. So, that brings us to...

The Implied Message of His Name

You see, all of those things that we just talked about, the inherent meaning of the word, most likely tell us a lot about this man. Think about it. He was probably...

Younger. He had two brothers, one named Matthew and the other named Joseph? Well, if you take what his name means, then this was probably "little James." Maybe he was the baby of the family.

Smaller. Hebert Lockyer says that a good way to translate his name is "James, the little." Maybe he was on the short side. Maybe he was a lot like Zacchaeus.

Weaker. If you put those first two things together then it's easy to see that compared to the older, bigger guys around him that he could have been weaker.

And then lastly, we're probably talking about a man who had...

Less influence of status. As a matter of fact, let me show you something that I think is really telling about his position in this group of twelve.

Matthew 10:2–3

"Now the names of the twelve apostles are these; The first, Simon, who is called Peter, and Andrew his brother; James the son of Zabedee, and John his brother; Philip, and Bartholomew; Thomas, and Matthew the publican; James the son of Alphaeus, and Lebbaeus, whose surname was Thaddaeus;"

Mark 3:14–19

"And he ordained twelve, that they should be with him, and that he might send them forth to preach, And to have power to heal sicknesses, and to cast out devils: And Simon he surnamed Peter; And James the son of Zebedee, and John the brother of James; and he surnamed them Boanerges, which is, The sons of thunder: And Andrew, and Philip, and Bartholomew, and Matthew, and Thomas, and James the son of Alphaeius, and Thaddaeus, and Simon the Canaanite, and Judas Iscariot, which also betrayed him: and they went into an house."

Luke 6:13–16

"And when it was day, he called unto him his disciples: and of them he chose twelve, whom also he named apostles; Simon, whom he also named Peter,) and Andrew his brother, James and John, Philip and Bartholomew, Matthew and Thomas, James the son of Alphaeus, and Simon called Zelotes, And Judas the brother of James, and Judas Iscariot, which also was the traitor."

Acts 1:13

"And when they were come in, they went up into an upper room, where abode both Peter, and James, and John, and Andrew, Philip, and Thomas, Bartholomew, and Matthew, James the son of Alphaeus, and Simon Zelotes, and Judas the brother of James."

You see, whenever and wherever these twelve men are listed, James the less is always in that last group, right before the traitor.

So, there's the inherent meaning of his name. Then there's the implied message of his name, and then thirdly, and this is where the message is, there's...

The Important Motivation of His Name

Let me ask you a question, how would you feel if at the end of your life on earth, the only specific mention about you was you first name? I mean, nobody knew when you were born, where you were from, what you had done, how you had died; the only thing that they knew about you was that at about this point in history there was a person named John or Joe or Sally or Susan, how would that make you feel? Well, that's what happened to James. No wonder John MacArthur calls James "the obscure disciple." We're not told about his birth. We're not told about his accomplishments. We're not even told about his death. Unlike most of the other disciples, history can't even agree with how he died. Some accounts say that he was stoned; others say that he was beaten to death; and still others say that he was crucified like Jesus. And yet, here he is listed with a group of men that the Bible says turned the whole world upside down.

Do you know what that teaches me? It teaches me that...

Little is much when God is in it. Do you know how many times the word "big" is used in the Bible? Zero. The word "little" is used almost 250 times in the Bible. That ought to tell you something. What we think of being big and what the Lord thinks of being big are two entirely different things. And God in His greatness and God in His wisdom, the Bible says, has chosen to use the small things, the insignificant things, the little things, and the lesser things of this world to accomplish the things that He wants to accomplish.

You say, "Pastor, I can only give a little, or serve a little or teach a little–remember, little is much when God is in it. Take this whole matter of giving. Did you know that there's a story in the Bible about a widow woman who came and gave just two pennies to God, while those around her gave hundreds and thousands of dollars, and do you know what Jesus said? He said, *"I'm telling you that this poor widow has put in more than all those who have given to the treasury; for they all put in out of their abundance, but she out of her poverty put in all that she had, her whole livelihood."*

You say, "Pastor, I can only serve a little." I don't have the ability to teach a class. I don't have the experience to serve on a committee. I don't have the boldness to go up to a complete stranger and tell them about Jesus. All I can do is welcome people into the church." Do you know what David said? *"I'd rather be a doorkeeper in the House of my God than to dwell in the tents of the wicked."*

I could go on and on, but the point is, little is much when God is in it.

There's an old gospel song with those words:

> "Little is much when God is in it.
>
> labor not, for wealth or fame.
>
> There's a prize, and you can win it,
>
> If you'll go in Jesus' name."

Here's the last thing.

Unrecognized does not mean unrewarded.
Revelation 21:14
"And the wall of the city had twelve foundations, and in them the names of the twelve apostles of the Lamb."

As you can see, James was eventually rewarded. I assure you that God will reward you one day for the things you do for Him.

e|LIVE

listen|imagine|view|experience

AUDIO BOOK DOWNLOAD INCLUDED WITH THIS BOOK!

In your hands you hold a complete digital entertainment package. Besides purchasing the paper version of this book, this book includes a free download of the audio version of this book. Simply use the code listed below when visiting our website. Once downloaded to your computer, you can listen to the book through your computer's speakers, burn it to an audio CD or save the file to your portable music device (such as Apple's popular iPod) and listen on the go!

How to get your free audio book digital download:

1. Visit www.tatepublishing.com and click on the e|LIVE logo on the home page.
2. Enter the following coupon code:
   6a01-8115-8e0c-fd6e-4ace-de56-ac75-cf55
3. Download the audio book from your e|LIVE digital locker and begin enjoying your new digital entertainment package today!